The One l

A Beautiful Big Explainer

Gene Haley

Table of Contents

INTRODUCTION

On July 3, 2025, the United States Congress passed a piece of legislation with a name as ambitious as its scope: the "One Big Beautiful Bill." Set against the backdrop of a deeply divided nation, this bill, often referred to by its acronym OBBB, represents one of the most significant and wide-ranging legislative packages in recent American history. Spanning over a thousand pages, it proposes a fundamental reshaping of the nation's tax code, social safety nets, energy policy, and national security priorities. This book, "The One Big Beautiful Bill: A Beautiful Big Explainer," is designed to be your guide through this complex and consequential legislation. Our goal is to provide a clear, straightforward, and unbiased explanation of what the OBBB contains, how it came to be, and what it could mean for you, your family, and the country as a whole.

The journey of the One Big Beautiful Bill through the halls of Congress was nothing short of a political drama. Introduced in the House of Representatives on May 16, 2025, by Representative Jodey Arrington, it was fast-tracked using the budget reconciliation process. This procedural maneuver allowed the bill to bypass the Senate's filibuster rule, requiring only a simple majority for passage. Even with this advantage, the bill's passage was a nail-biting affair, highlighting the razor-thin margins in both chambers of Congress. The House initially passed the bill on May 22, 2025, with a vote of 215-214, with one member voting present. The bill then moved to the Senate, where it underwent significant revisions and a marathon 27-hour debate. Ultimately, on July 1, 2025, the Senate passed its amended version with a 51-50 vote, the tie broken by Vice President JD Vance. The amended bill was then sent back to the House, which, after intense last-minute negotiations and personal appeals from the President, passed the final version on July 3, 2025, by a vote of 218-214.

At its core, the One Big Beautiful Bill is a reflection of a particular political and economic philosophy. It champions lower taxes, reduced government spending on social programs, a bolstered national defense, and a renewed focus on domestic energy production. The bill's proponents argue that it will unleash economic growth, create jobs, and provide financial relief to working families. They point to provisions that make the Trump-era tax cuts permanent, eliminate taxes on tips and overtime for many workers, and expand the child tax credit as evidence of the bill's focus on the middle class. Furthermore, they contend that the bill's increased funding for the military and border security will make the nation safer and more secure.

On the other hand, critics of the OBBB paint a starkly different picture. They argue that the bill's tax cuts disproportionately benefit the wealthy and corporations, while the spending cuts will harm the most vulnerable Americans. Concerns have been raised about the significant reductions in funding for programs like Medicaid and the Supplemental Nutrition Assistance Program (SNAP), with opponents claiming these cuts will leave millions without access to essential services. The Congressional Budget Office, a nonpartisan agency, has estimated that the bill will add trillions of dollars to the national debt over the next decade. There are also deep divisions over the bill's environmental provisions, which roll back clean energy tax credits and promote the use of fossil fuels.

This book will delve into the specifics of each of these major policy areas, providing a detailed yet accessible explanation of the changes enacted by the OBBB. We will explore the extension of the 2017 Tax Cuts and Jobs Act, breaking down what it means for individual taxpayers, families, and businesses of all sizes. We will examine the new tax breaks, such as the elimination of taxes on tips and overtime, and the expanded child tax credit, explaining who is eligible and how these provisions will work. The book will also provide a thorough analysis of the changes to the estate tax and the State and Local Tax (SALT) deduction, issues of great importance to many American families.

Beyond taxes, this book will guide you through the significant reforms to the nation's social safety net. We will explain the new work requirements and eligibility rules for the Supplemental Nutrition Assistance Program (SNAP) and the far-reaching overhaul of Medicaid. These changes are among the most controversial aspects of the OBBB, and we will present the arguments from both sides of the debate, allowing you to draw your own conclusions about their potential impact.

The One Big Beautiful Bill also represents a major shift in the nation's priorities when it comes to national security and defense. This book will detail the massive boost in funding for the military, as well as the resources allocated for improving the quality of life for service members and their families. We will also provide a comprehensive overview of the bill's immigration provisions, including the surge in funding for border security and the implementation of a nationwide deportation initiative.

In the realm of energy and the environment, the OBBB marks a significant departure from the policies of the previous administration. This book will explain the end of many green energy tax credits and the new emphasis on domestic oil, gas, and coal production. We will also explore the bill's impact on American agriculture, with a look at the new subsidies and support for farmers.

The OBBB's influence extends to nearly every facet of American life, and this book will cover these diverse areas in detail. We will examine the bill's provisions related to "America First" technology and innovation, the future of education funding and school choice, and the changes to transportation and infrastructure priorities. The book will also tackle the complex issue of the national debt, explaining how the OBBB affects the debt ceiling and the long-term economic outlook.

To provide a complete picture, this book will also explore the political story behind the OBBB, offering insights into the legislative maneuvering and deal-making that led to its passage. We will look at the winners and losers in major industries and what the bill means for the average American household. Finally, we will consider the broader implications of the One Big Beautiful Bill and its potential to shape the future of the country.

Navigating a piece of legislation as vast and complex as the OBBB can be a daunting task. The language of law is often dense and inaccessible to the layperson, filled with jargon and technical details that can obscure the real-world consequences of the policies being enacted. This book aims to bridge that gap. We have taken the full text of the bill, available at congress.gov, and translated it into plain, understandable English. Our goal is not to tell you what to think about the OBBB, but to provide you with the information you need to understand it for yourself. Whether you are a student, a business owner, a parent, or simply a concerned citizen, this book is for you. Welcome to "The One Big Beautiful Bill: A Beautiful Big Explainer."

Note:

A copy of the full text of the bill can be found at:

https://www.congress.gov/bill/119th-congress/house-bill/1/text

CHAPTER ONE: The "One Big Beautiful Bill": An Overview

Welcome to the heart of the matter. The One Big Beautiful Bill, or OBBB, is not just a piece of legislation; it's a statement of intent, a roadmap for a different direction for the country. To truly grasp its significance, one must look beyond the partisan cheering and jeering that accompanied its tumultuous passage. Think of this chapter as your bird's-eye view, a guided tour from 30,000 feet before we parachute into the dense forests of its specific provisions in the chapters to come. The bill is a sprawling legislative mosaic, piecing together vast changes in taxation, social welfare, national defense, immigration, and energy policy. Its architects bundled these disparate elements into a single, massive package using the budget reconciliation process, a legislative fast-track that bypasses the Senate filibuster and allows for passage with a simple majority. This procedural choice is key to understanding not only how the bill passed, but why it is so broad in its ambitions.

At its core, the OBBB is built on a distinct philosophy that champions a smaller role for the federal government in some areas and a vastly expanded role in others. The central pillars of this philosophy are clear: significantly lower taxes for individuals and corporations, a reduction in spending on social safety net programs, a major reinvestment in the nation's military and defense capabilities, and a strategic pivot in energy policy toward fossil fuels. Proponents argue this combination will ignite economic growth, unshackle American businesses, provide financial relief to families, and secure the nation's borders and global interests. Critics, however, see a formula that deepens inequality, shreds essential social supports, exacerbates the national debt, and reverses progress on environmental protection. This fundamental disagreement is the friction point around which the entire debate over the OBBB revolves.

The most prominent feature of the bill, and the one that will likely touch the most lives directly, is its sweeping tax reform. The legislation makes the individual tax rate cuts first enacted in the 2017 Tax Cuts and Jobs Act permanent, preventing a scheduled tax increase for millions of Americans. Beyond this extension, the bill introduces several new, targeted tax breaks. These include novel deductions for income earned from tips and overtime for many workers, aiming to provide relief to hourly and service-industry employees. For businesses, the bill restores and enhances provisions allowing for the immediate write-off of investments in new equipment and research, a policy intended to spur capital investment and innovation. These changes represent a significant and permanent restructuring of the American tax code, the full implications of which we will explore in detail.

For families, the OBBB brings notable changes to how the government provides support. A key provision is the permanent increase of the Child Tax Credit to $2,200, with the amount indexed to inflation for future years. This aims to provide more financial breathing room for parents. The bill also tackles the controversial State and Local Tax (SALT) deduction. In a significant shift, the cap on this deduction is raised from $10,000 to $40,000 for five years for most taxpayers, a measure that will primarily benefit residents of high-tax states. Another area of focus is the federal estate tax, often dubbed the "death tax" by its opponents. The OBBB permanently increases the exemption amount to $15 million per person, shielding more family farms and businesses from being taxed when passed to the next generation.

While the bill provides tax relief in many areas, it enacts significant reforms and spending reductions in the nation's social safety net. The Supplemental Nutrition Assistance Program (SNAP), which provides food aid to low-income individuals and families, will see the implementation of stricter work requirements for able-bodied adults without dependents. Similarly, the OBBB initiates a major overhaul of Medicaid, the joint federal and state program that provides health coverage to millions of low-income Americans. The legislation introduces work requirements for some Medicaid recipients for the first time and alters the program's funding structure. Proponents argue these changes are necessary to ensure the long-term sustainability of these programs and to encourage work. Opponents counter that they will result in millions losing access to essential food and healthcare services.

A dramatic shift in federal priorities is also evident in the bill's approach to national security and immigration. The legislation authorizes a substantial increase in the national defense budget, allocating hundreds of billions of dollars toward military modernization, readiness, and improved quality of life for service members. This boost in spending reflects a core objective of the bill: to project American strength on the global stage. Complementing the military spending is a massive new investment in border security. The bill allocates tens of billions of dollars for the construction of a border wall, the hiring of thousands of new immigration enforcement agents, and the expansion of detention facilities. It also funds a nationwide initiative aimed at significantly increasing the number of deportations of undocumented immigrants.

In the realm of energy and the environment, the OBBB marks a decisive break from the policies of recent years. The bill accelerates the phase-out of numerous tax credits for clean and renewable energy sources, such as wind, solar, and electric vehicles, which were central to the previous administration's climate agenda. The legislation also repeals fees on methane emissions and takes steps to unlock more oil and gas development on federal lands. This "unleashing" of American energy, as its supporters call it, is designed to lower energy costs and re-establish American energy dominance through a renewed focus on oil, gas, and coal. This pivot away from green energy incentives is one of the most contentious elements of the bill, sparking intense debate about the nation's economic and environmental future.

Beyond these major pillars, the OBBB extends its reach into nearly every corner of American policy. It contains significant new subsidies and supports for farmers, aiming to bolster the nation's agricultural sector. It establishes new funding priorities for technology and innovation, with an emphasis on an "America First" approach. The bill also signals changes in federal education policy, including a new tax credit to encourage donations to private school voucher funds, a move intended to promote school choice. Even infrastructure priorities are reshaped, reflecting the new governing philosophy. Understanding the OBBB requires an appreciation for this immense scope; it is not a bill that tinkers at the margins but one that attempts a fundamental reordering of federal policy.

The very structure of the bill as a single, all-encompassing package is itself a major part of the story. By bundling popular items like tax cuts with more controversial measures like social program reforms and fossil fuel incentives, the bill's authors created a legislative vehicle that was difficult for lawmakers to oppose in its entirety. This "omnibus" approach, while politically effective, has been criticized for a lack of transparency and for forcing members of Congress to vote on a wide array of policies with a single "yes" or "no." The bill's journey through Congress, reliant on the tie-breaking vote of the Vice President in the Senate, underscores the deep partisan divisions that define modern American politics.

Finally, any overview of the OBBB would be incomplete without acknowledging its significant fiscal impact. According to the non-partisan Congressional Budget Office (CBO), the combination of sweeping tax cuts and increased defense spending is projected to add trillions of dollars to the national debt over the next decade. The bill's proponents argue that the economic growth spurred by the tax cuts will ultimately generate enough new revenue to offset this deficit, a concept known as "dynamic scoring." However, this remains a subject of intense debate among economists, and the bill's long-term effect on the nation's fiscal health will be a critical measure of its success or failure.

This chapter has provided the broad strokes of the One Big Beautiful Bill. We've seen its philosophical underpinnings and taken a high-level tour of its main components: tax cuts, social program overhauls, defense spending, border security, and energy policy shifts. The purpose was to equip you with a foundational understanding of what this legislation is and what it aims to do.

Now, with this framework in place, we are ready to move beyond the overview and delve into the specific details. The following chapters will take each of these major policy areas and break them down, piece by piece, so you can understand not just the headlines, but the fine print that will shape the lives of Americans for years to come.

CHAPTER TWO: Making the Trump-Era Tax Cuts Permanent

To understand one of the biggest and most immediate impacts of the One Big Beautiful Bill, we need to hop in a time machine and travel back to the year 2017. That was the year Congress passed the Tax Cuts and Jobs Act, or TCJA, a piece of legislation that fundamentally rewrote the American tax code. It was a massive bill that lowered tax rates for most individuals and slashed the tax burden on corporations. However, it was built with a ticking clock. To comply with complex Senate budget rules, nearly all the changes affecting individual taxpayers were designed to be temporary. They were set to automatically "sunset," or expire, at the end of 2025.

For years, this expiration date loomed over households and financial planners like a gathering storm cloud. If Congress did nothing, millions of Americans would have woken up on January 1, 2026, to a completely different tax reality—one that looked a lot more like the pre-2018 system, with higher tax rates, a smaller standard deduction, and the disappearance of several popular tax breaks. This scenario was often referred to as a "fiscal cliff," a sudden and significant tax hike for the vast majority of taxpayers. The One Big Beautiful Bill essentially marches right up to that cliff edge and builds a permanent bridge across it. Its primary tax provision is to take those temporary individual tax cuts from the TCJA and chisel them into the bedrock of the U.S. tax code.

The most direct change involves the income tax brackets that determine how much of your paycheck goes to Uncle Sam. The TCJA established seven tax brackets with lower rates than the system they replaced: 10%, 12%, 22%, 24%, 32%, 35%, and 37%. Without the OBBB, the tax code would have snapped back to the old structure in 2026, which had brackets of 10%, 15%, 25%, 28%, 33%, 35%, and a top rate of 39.6%. For most people, this would have meant paying a higher percentage of their income in taxes. The OBBB prevents this by making the seven-bracket structure from the TCJA the law of the land, indefinitely.

Let's consider a simple, hypothetical example. Imagine a married couple filing jointly with a taxable income of $150,000 in 2026. Under the old system that was scheduled to return, they would find themselves in the 25% bracket. Under the TCJA rates, which the OBBB now makes permanent, that same income level falls into the 22% bracket. While a 3% difference might not sound like much, it translates into thousands of dollars in tax savings year after year. Proponents of the OBBB argue that this provides crucial certainty and financial relief, allowing families to keep more of their hard-earned money to save, spend, or invest as they see fit. They see it not as a tax cut, but as the prevention of a massive, automatic tax increase.

Of course, tax rates are only part of the equation. The other seismic shift from the TCJA that the OBBB makes permanent is the vastly increased standard deduction. Think of the standard deduction as a flat-dollar amount that you can subtract from your income to reduce the amount that is subject to tax. Before 2018, taxpayers could either take the standard deduction or they could "itemize" their deductions—a complicated process of adding up specific expenses like mortgage interest, charitable giving, and certain medical costs. The TCJA dramatically simplified this for millions of people by nearly doubling the size of the standard deduction.

This had a profound effect on tax preparation. Suddenly, for tens of millions of households, the new, larger standard deduction was greater than the sum of all their potential itemized deductions. This meant they no longer needed to go through the headache and expense of tracking receipts and filling out extra forms; they could simply take the standard deduction and be done with it. It was a change celebrated for its simplicity. However, like the lower tax rates, this enlarged standard deduction was also on the track to expire, scheduled to be cut roughly in half in 2026. The OBBB steps in and makes the higher standard deduction permanent, ensuring that this simplified path to filing remains available.

There is, however, another side to this particular coin. To help pay for the larger standard deduction, the TCJA eliminated the personal exemption. This was a feature of the old tax code that allowed you to deduct a certain amount of money for yourself, your spouse, and each of your dependents. It was a significant tax break, especially for larger families. The logic of the TCJA was that the larger standard deduction, combined with an expanded Child Tax Credit, would more than make up for the loss of the personal exemption for most families. The OBBB, by making the TCJA's individual provisions permanent, also permanently eliminates the personal exemption, solidifying this fundamental trade-off in the tax code.

Beyond the provisions that affect almost every taxpayer, the OBBB also cements a critical tax break for small and medium-sized businesses. The 2017 TCJA created a brand-new deduction, officially known as Section 199A, but more commonly called the Qualified Business Income (QBI) deduction. This was a lifeline for so-called "pass-through" businesses—entities like sole proprietorships, partnerships, S corporations, and LLCs, where the business profits "pass through" to the owner's personal tax return and are taxed at individual rates. This covers a huge swath of the American economy, from the local plumber and corner bakery to freelance consultants and family-owned farms.

The QBI deduction allowed these business owners to deduct up to 20% of their qualified business income, effectively lowering their tax rate and allowing them to keep more capital in their businesses to hire, expand, and invest. It was a complex and sometimes confusing deduction, with various income thresholds and limitations, but it was also one of the most significant pieces of tax relief for "Main Street" businesses in the entire TCJA. Unsurprisingly, it too was on the chopping block, set to vanish completely after 2025. The OBBB reverses this, making the 20% pass-through deduction a permanent fixture. For proponents, this is a cornerstone of the bill's pro-growth agenda, providing long-term certainty for entrepreneurs and business owners.

It is important to clarify one common point of confusion regarding the corporate tax changes. While the TCJA's individual tax cuts were temporary, its centerpiece—the reduction of the top corporate tax rate from 35% down to a flat 21%—was made permanent from the start. Therefore, the OBBB did not need to act to preserve this lower rate for large, traditional C-corporations; it was already the law. However, the OBBB does provide a significant and permanent boost for business investment through another TCJA provision known as bonus depreciation.

In simple terms, bonus depreciation allows a business to immediately deduct a large percentage of the purchase price of eligible assets, like machinery, equipment, and vehicles, rather than writing them off slowly over many years. The TCJA took this concept and put it on steroids, allowing for 100% bonus depreciation. This meant a company could deduct the full cost of a new piece of equipment in the year it was bought, providing a powerful incentive to invest in upgrading their operations. However, this 100% provision began to phase down after 2022, dropping to 80% in 2023, 60% in 2024, and so on, until it disappeared. The OBBB reverses this phase-out, restoring 100% bonus depreciation and making it a permanent policy, a move supporters claim will be a major catalyst for domestic manufacturing and technological advancement.

The permanence of the TCJA's framework also serves as the foundation for other major changes detailed later in this book. For instance, the 2017 law doubled the Child Tax Credit from $1,000 to $2,000 per child and made more of it refundable, but this, too, was a temporary change. As we will explore in Chapter 4, the OBBB not only makes that increase permanent but expands upon it significantly. Similarly, the TCJA doubled the amount of wealth that could be passed down to heirs without triggering the federal estate tax, a provision that was set to revert to its lower, pre-2018 level. As Chapter 6 will detail, the OBBB locks in this higher exemption and increases it further.

The bill also addresses one of the most controversial elements of the TCJA: the $10,000 cap on the deduction for state and local taxes, or SALT. This provision was a major blow to taxpayers in high-tax states like New York, New Jersey, and California, and it was also scheduled to expire with the rest of the individual cuts. The OBBB doesn't just make the cap permanent; it fundamentally alters it, a complex story we will unravel completely in Chapter 7. By making the core of the TCJA permanent, the OBBB creates a stable, long-term baseline from which to launch these other, more targeted policy changes.

As with any legislation of this magnitude, making the Trump-era tax cuts permanent has been the subject of fierce debate. Proponents of the OBBB frame the move as an act of vital economic stewardship. They argue that allowing the cuts to expire would have constituted the largest tax increase in recent American history, hitting middle-class families and small businesses the hardest. In their view, permanence provides stability and predictability. Families can confidently plan their financial futures, and businesses, freed from the uncertainty of a looming tax hike, are more likely to make the long-term investments that create jobs and drive economic growth. The promise is that a simpler, lower, and more stable tax code will unleash the full potential of the American economy.

On the other side of the ledger, critics of the OBBB point to the enormous cost of making these tax cuts permanent. Independent analysis from the non-partisan Congressional Budget Office, which was cited frequently during the bill's debate, projected that extending the cuts would add trillions of dollars to the national debt over the next decade. Opponents argue that this is a fiscally reckless path, placing an unsustainable burden on future generations. They also contend that the benefits of the TCJA were not evenly distributed, with a disproportionate share of the tax savings flowing to corporations and the wealthiest households. By making these provisions permanent, critics say, the OBBB locks in a tax structure that exacerbates income inequality and starves the government of revenue needed for critical public services like healthcare, education, and infrastructure.

CHAPTER THREE: No More Taxes on Tips and Overtime

Of all the changes packed into the One Big Beautiful Bill, few are as direct, as easy to understand, and as potentially impactful for millions of working Americans as the provisions targeting tips and overtime pay. For generations, the rule has been simple: if you earn it, Uncle Sam gets a piece of it. Whether that income came from your hourly wage, a sales commission, a holiday bonus, or the extra cash a customer left on the table for great service, it was all considered taxable income. The OBBB redraws this fundamental line in the sand. It creates two brand-new, powerful tax exemptions aimed squarely at the paychecks of service industry staff, factory workers, nurses, tradespeople, and countless others who rely on gratuities or extra hours to make ends meet.

The concept is strikingly straightforward: for the first time, the federal government will no longer levy income tax on money earned from tips or from working overtime. This is not a deduction or a credit, which only reduces the amount of income subject to tax or the final tax bill. This is an outright exemption. The money is yours to keep, free and clear from federal income tax. Imagine a world where the cash you collect at the end of a long shift as a waiter or bartender is treated differently by the taxman than your base hourly wage. Or picture a scenario where the extra money you earn for taking on a weekend shift doesn't get hit by taxes at all. That is the new reality the OBBB creates.

Let's start with the first part of this duo: the elimination of federal income tax on tips. To appreciate the scale of this change, you have to understand the old system. Previously, any tips an employee received were considered part of their wages. This applied whether it was cash left on the table, a gratuity added to a credit card slip, or a tip paid out from a tip pool. The Internal Revenue Service (IRS) required employees to report all of their tip income to their employer, who would then include it in their wages for tax purposes. That meant tips were subject to the same taxes as your regular paycheck: federal income tax, Social Security tax, and Medicare tax.

The OBBB completely upends the federal income tax part of that equation. Under the new law, all reported tip income is now 100% exempt from federal income taxation. There are no income limits and no caps on the amount of tips that can be excluded. If a bartender earns $20,000 a year in base wages and an additional $40,000 in tips, only the $20,000 in wages will be subject to federal income tax. The $40,000 in tips, while still needing to be reported, will not have a single dollar of federal income tax withheld from it or owed on it when it's time to file a tax return in April.

It is crucial, however, to highlight a very important piece of the fine print. The exemption applies only to *federal income tax*. Tips are still considered earnings for the purpose of Social Security and Medicare taxes, often referred to as FICA taxes. This is a critical distinction. The 7.65% that employees pay into these programs (and the matching 7.65% from their employers) will still be calculated based on the total of wages plus tips. The logic behind this is that these programs provide benefits—retirement income and healthcare in old age—that are based on a lifetime of earnings. To exclude tips from this calculation would mean lower future Social Security benefits for millions of tipped workers, something the bill's architects sought to avoid.

The new rule applies broadly to any employee who customarily and regularly receives tips. The long-standing IRS definition is generally used here, which covers workers who receive more than $30 per month in tips. This encompasses a massive and diverse workforce, including restaurant servers, bartenders, hair stylists, nail technicians, hotel bellhops, valets, casino dealers, and delivery drivers. The proponents of this change championed it as a matter of fairness and economic stimulus. They argued that tips are not a wage paid by an employer, but a voluntary gift from a customer to reward good service. Taxing these gratuities, they contended, was fundamentally unfair.

The political sales pitch for this provision was one of the easiest and most effective of the entire OBBB. It was framed as a direct tax cut for the little guy, the hard-working American who is on their feet all day. The promise was simple: this change will immediately increase the take-home pay of millions, providing much-needed financial relief in a time of rising costs. For a server or stylist, this could mean hundreds or even thousands of dollars more in their pocket each year, money that could be used for groceries, rent, or saving for a child's education. The argument was that this money would be spent almost immediately in local economies, creating a ripple effect of economic activity.

Of course, the proposal did not sail through without debate. Critics raised several important concerns. First and foremost was the cost. Eliminating a stream of tax revenue, no matter how popular, has a budgetary impact. Opponents pointed to estimates that this single provision would reduce federal revenues by tens of billions of dollars over the next decade, adding to the national debt. They argued that while the benefit to individuals is clear, the collective cost to the nation's finances is substantial. This lost revenue, they claimed, would have to be made up by cutting spending on public services or by increasing the national debt that future generations must pay.

Another line of criticism focused on fairness and the potential for unintended consequences. The new law creates a significant tax advantage for workers in certain industries. A restaurant server, for example, will now have a large portion of their income tax-free, while a retail clerk or a childcare worker earning the exact same total amount, but entirely through wages, will pay income tax on all of it. This, critics argued, arbitrarily picks winners and losers in the labor market, creating a new and complicated wrinkle in the tax code. There were also concerns that some employers might see this as an opportunity to lower base wages for tipped staff, assuming that the new tax-free nature of tips would make up the difference, potentially leaving workers no better off.

The administrative side also presents new challenges. While employees were always supposed to report all tips, the new tax-free status creates a much stronger incentive to do so accurately. For employers, payroll systems must be reconfigured. They now have to meticulously track and separate three categories of income for each employee: regular wages (subject to all taxes), reported tips (subject only to FICA taxes), and, as we'll see next, overtime pay (also subject only to FICA taxes). This adds a new layer of complexity to what is already a daunting task for many small business owners. The W-2 form, the statement of annual earnings sent to every employee, will have to be redesigned to reflect these new categories of income.

The second major pillar of this chapter's topic is the new tax exemption for overtime pay. Much like the provision for tips, the OBBB carves out all income earned from overtime hours, making it completely exempt from federal income tax. The rule for decades has been that overtime pay—typically calculated at one-and-a-half times a worker's regular rate for any hours worked beyond 40 in a week—is taxed just like any other wage. In fact, because of the way tax withholding is calculated, a large overtime check could often feel like it was taxed at an even higher rate, as it could temporarily push an employee into a higher withholding bracket.

The OBBB changes this overnight. The new law applies to all overtime payments made to "non-exempt" employees, which is a legal term defined by the Fair Labor Standards Act (FLSA). In simple terms, non-exempt employees are those who are entitled to overtime pay, a category that includes most hourly workers in fields like manufacturing, construction, healthcare support, transportation, and administrative roles. For these workers, the extra money earned by staying late or coming in on a Saturday will no longer be diminished by federal income taxes.

Consider a hypothetical factory worker who earns $25 per hour. Her regular 40-hour week nets her $1,000 in gross pay. If she works an extra ten hours of overtime, she earns time-and-a-half, or $37.50 per hour, for that extra work. This adds $375 to her weekly paycheck. Before the OBBB, that entire $1,375 would have been subject to federal income tax. Now, only the first $1,000 is. The

$375 in overtime pay is hers to keep, untouched by the IRS. Just like with tips, this income remains subject to Social Security and Medicare taxes to ensure that workers continue to build credit toward their future retirement and healthcare benefits.

The arguments in favor of the overtime tax exemption closely mirrored those for the tip exemption. Proponents sold it as a direct reward for hard work and a powerful incentive for American productivity. The message was that the government should not be penalizing workers for their willingness to go the extra mile. By allowing employees to keep the full fruits of their extra labor, the bill would provide a significant boost to the earnings of millions of middle-class families. This was presented as a core component of the bill's "pro-worker" agenda, designed to help blue-collar workers get ahead.

The economic argument was that this policy would not only help individual families but also encourage a more dynamic labor market. With overtime being more financially attractive to employees, companies might find it easier to ramp up production to meet demand without the immediate need to hire and train new staff. For workers, it makes the decision to take on an extra shift much more appealing, directly translating into a bigger, tax-free addition to their take-home pay. This, supporters argued, is a common-sense policy that respects and rewards the dignity of work.

The criticisms of the overtime tax exemption also followed a similar pattern. The fiscal impact was a primary concern, with opponents highlighting the billions in lost tax revenue that would contribute to a rising national debt. They argued that the government simply could not afford to stop taxing such a significant category of earned income without making painful choices elsewhere. The debate over who benefits most was also central to the opposition's case. They pointed out that the provision does nothing for the millions of salaried workers who are "exempt" from overtime laws.

This creates a new disparity in the workforce. An exempt office manager who works 55 hours a week to meet a deadline receives no tax benefit for those extra 15 hours. Meanwhile, an hourly employee in the same company working the same number of extra hours would receive their overtime pay tax-free. Critics contended this was fundamentally inequitable. Furthermore, some economists and labor advocates warned that the policy could have a negative long-term effect on job creation. If it becomes significantly cheaper for a company to pay existing staff tax-advantaged overtime rather than hiring a new employee and paying benefits, the incentive to create new jobs could be diminished.

The practical implementation of this policy also requires significant adjustments from businesses. Payroll departments must now be able to precisely identify and isolate overtime hours and pay from regular hours and pay. For businesses that have complex pay structures, with varying shift differentials and premium pay, this could become an accounting headache. It requires a level of detail in payroll processing that many smaller firms may not be equipped to handle without investing in new software and training, adding to their administrative burden and compliance costs.

Together, these two provisions—the exemptions for tips and overtime—represent a fundamental rethinking of what constitutes "income" for tax purposes. They are targeted, highly visible tax cuts that deliver a direct and easily understood benefit to a broad cross-section of the American workforce. They are a departure from the complex web of deductions and credits that often characterize tax policy, offering instead a simple promise: the money you earn from tips and extra hours is yours, and the federal income tax collector can't touch it.

The inclusion of these policies in the One Big Beautiful Bill was a masterstroke of political messaging. It allowed the bill's sponsors to counter the narrative that their tax agenda was focused only on corporations and the wealthy. The "No Tax on Tips" slogan became a powerful rallying cry, resonating with anyone who has ever worked in a service job or knows someone who does. It provided a tangible, kitchen-table benefit that was easy to explain and hard to argue against in a soundbite. While economists and policy experts debated the long-term fiscal consequences and potential market distortions, the political appeal of letting working people keep more of their money proved to be overwhelmingly potent during the bill's journey through Congress.

CHAPTER FOUR: The New, Expanded Child Tax Credit

Among the most significant household finance provisions in the One Big Beautiful Bill is its ambitious overhaul of the Child Tax Credit, or CTC. For decades, this credit has been a feature of the tax code designed to help ease the financial burden of raising children. As we covered in Chapter Two, the 2017 Tax Cuts and Jobs Act (TCJA) temporarily doubled the credit from $1,000 to $2,000 per child, a change that was set to expire at the end of 2025. The OBBB not only prevents that from happening but builds upon that foundation, creating a more generous and permanent version of the credit.

The centerpiece of the OBBB's changes is a permanent increase in the maximum credit amount. The bill raises the credit from the TCJA's $2,000 to a new baseline of $2,200 for each qualifying child under the age of 17. This represents a direct, dollar-for-dollar reduction in the federal income taxes a family owes. For a married couple with three eligible children, this change alone translates into an additional $600 in tax relief each year compared to the expiring law, bringing their total credit to $6,600.

Perhaps more significant in the long run, the OBBB introduces a new feature to the credit: it will be indexed to inflation. This is a crucial detail that distinguishes this new version from all its predecessors. Indexing for inflation means the value of the credit will automatically increase over time to keep pace with the rising cost of living. Without this feature, a tax provision with a fixed dollar amount, like the old CTC, loses a little bit of its purchasing power every year as prices for goods and services go up.

Here is how it works in practice: each year, the Treasury Department will look at a specific measure of inflation, likely the Consumer Price Index, and adjust the value of the credit accordingly. So, if inflation runs at 3% in a given year, the $2,200 credit would be adjusted upward for the following year to maintain its real value. This prevents the slow erosion of the benefit over time and ensures that the financial support it provides to families does not diminish simply because of normal economic price increases.

The bill's authors argued that indexing the credit provides families with much-needed predictability. Parents can plan their long-term finances with the confidence that the value of this crucial tax benefit won't be chipped away by inflation. It transforms the CTC from a static number into a dynamic form of support that adapts to the economic environment, a key feature in an era of fluctuating prices for essentials like groceries, childcare, and clothing.

To receive the credit, families must meet a set of well-established criteria. First, the child must be under the age of 17 at the end of the tax year. They must also be your son, daughter, stepchild, eligible foster child, brother, sister, or a descendant of any of these individuals, such as a grandchild. The child must have lived with you for more than half the year and must not have provided more than half of their own financial support.

A critical eligibility requirement retained and made permanent by the OBBB is that the child must have a valid Social Security Number (SSN). This provision was first introduced by the TCJA and was a point of contention. It means that children who are U.S. citizens or residents but who do not have an SSN, such as those who might have an Individual Taxpayer Identification Number (ITIN), are not eligible for the $2,200 credit. This rule was designed to ensure the credit is directed only to families with children who are authorized to work in the United States.

The OBBB maintains the high income thresholds established by the TCJA, making the credit available to a broad swath of middle- and upper-middle-class families. The credit begins to phase out, or gradually decrease, for individuals with a modified adjusted gross income (MAGI) above $200,000 and for married couples filing jointly with a MAGI above $400,000. These thresholds are notably not indexed for inflation, meaning that over time, as wages rise, more families could find themselves entering the phase-out range.

The phase-out mechanism works by reducing the total credit amount by $50 for every $1,000 (or fraction thereof) that a taxpayer's income exceeds the threshold. For example, a married couple with one child and an income of $410,000 would see their $2,200 credit reduced by $500 (50 dollars for each of the ten thousand-dollar increments above $400,000), leaving them with a credit of $1,700. A family's credit is completely eliminated once their income is high enough to wipe it out entirely.

One of the most complex and debated aspects of the Child Tax Credit has always been its "refundability." A non-refundable tax credit can only be used to reduce your tax liability to zero. If your credit is larger than the taxes you owe, you simply don't get the rest. A refundable credit, on the other hand, means that if the credit is more than your tax bill, the government will send you the difference as a cash payment, or refund. This feature is especially important for low-income families who may owe very little or no federal income tax.

The TCJA made a portion of the credit—up to $1,400 in its first year, a figure that was indexed for inflation and had risen to $1,700 by 2025—refundable for families with earned income. The One Big Beautiful Bill makes this structure permanent but opts not to expand it further in the manner of the temporary 2021 changes. The bill locks in the maximum refundable portion of the credit at $1,400 per child, which will continue to be indexed for inflation moving forward.

To qualify for this refundable portion, known officially as the Additional Child Tax Credit (ACTC), a family must have earned income of at least $2,500. The amount of the refundable credit then "phases in" at a rate of 15 cents for every dollar earned above that $2,500 threshold, up to the maximum refundable amount. This structure is intended to tie the benefit to work.

Let's look at a hypothetical case. Consider a single mother with one child who works part-time and earns $15,000 a year. Her income is low enough that she owes no federal income tax. To calculate her refundable credit, we first subtract the $2,500 earnings threshold from her income ($15,000 - $2,500 = $12,500). We then multiply that amount by the 15% phase-in rate ($12,500 x 0.15 = $1,875). Because this amount is greater than the maximum refundable portion (which we will assume is $1,700 for the year), she would receive a tax refund of $1,700.

This earned-income requirement and the cap on refundability were central to the philosophy behind the OBBB's design of the credit. Proponents argued that these features ensure the CTC acts as a pro-work family benefit, rewarding and encouraging labor force participation. They contended that making the credit fully refundable without an earnings requirement, as was done temporarily in 2021, could discourage work by providing government payments with no strings attached, a point that has been debated by economists.

Critics of this approach, however, argued that this design leaves behind the children in the very poorest families. A family with no earned income, perhaps because a parent lost a job, is facing a severe illness, or is a full-time caregiver for another family member, would not be eligible to receive any of the refundable credit. Opponents pointed out that this structure means that millions of the nation's most vulnerable children would receive less benefit than those in families with higher earnings.

Another major policy decision within the OBBB was how the credit would be delivered to families. During the 2021 expansion, the IRS was directed to send out half of the credit as advance monthly payments, providing a steady stream of income to families throughout the year rather than a single lump sum at tax time. This experiment with monthly payments proved popular with many recipients but was also complex to administer.

The One Big Beautiful Bill rejects the monthly payment model and solidifies the traditional delivery mechanism. Families will receive the entire Child Tax Credit as they always have: as a single lump sum when they file their annual tax return. Proponents of this method argued it is simpler for the IRS to manage and avoids the potential for overpayments that can occur with advance systems if a family's income or circumstances change during the year.

Some families also prefer the lump-sum method, viewing their tax refund as a key moment for household savings or for making large, necessary purchases. On the other hand, advocates for monthly payments argued that a steady, predictable payment stream is more effective at helping low-income families meet their regular expenses like rent and groceries and can prevent them from falling into debt. The OBBB's choice to stick with the annual payment system represents a clear preference for administrative simplicity over this alternative model of support.

The OBBB also addresses the so-called "family penalty" in the tax code by maintaining a provision from the TCJA. Before 2018, the income phase-out for the CTC was significantly lower for married couples than for two single individuals, effectively penalizing some parents for getting married. The TCJA largely fixed this by setting the married-filing-jointly threshold at exactly double the single-filer threshold ($400,000 vs. $200,000), and the OBBB makes this structure permanent.

The debate around the expanded Child Tax Credit was one of the most passionate during the bill's passage. Supporters hailed it as a landmark investment in American families. They argued that by increasing the amount of the credit and, crucially, indexing it to inflation, the OBBB provides meaningful, lasting relief to help parents with the ever-increasing costs of raising children. This, they claimed, would not only improve family finances but would also boost the economy as parents spend the extra money on necessities.

Opponents, while generally supportive of helping families, raised significant concerns about the overall cost. Making the expanded credit permanent, even without some of the more ambitious proposals for full refundability, adds a substantial amount to the national debt over the next decade. Critics argued that the country could not afford such a large, permanent expenditure and that the money could be better targeted to families most in need, rather than providing a credit to households earning as much as $400,000 a year.

Furthermore, the debate over refundability and work requirements touches on a fundamental disagreement about the purpose of the credit. One side sees it as a tool to reduce child poverty, and from that perspective, it should be available to all children, regardless of their parents' work status. The other side views it as a way to lower the tax burden on working families, believing that tying the benefit to earned income is essential to promote self-sufficiency and avoid creating a disincentive to work. The OBBB's final version clearly lands on the side of the latter philosophy.

CHAPTER FIVE: Tax Breaks for Small Businesses and Entrepreneurs

While the permanent extension of the Qualified Business Income (QBI) deduction and 100% bonus depreciation, which we covered in Chapter Two, formed the bedrock of the One Big Beautiful Bill's business tax policy, the legislation did not stop there. The bill's architects included a suite of new and enhanced tax incentives aimed directly at the heart of the American economy: its small businesses and aspiring entrepreneurs. These provisions were designed not just to lower the tax burden on existing "Main Street" businesses, but to actively encourage the creation of new ones and reward those who take the financial risks associated with innovation and growth.

The philosophy behind this part of the bill was clear: while large corporations might have teams of accountants and lawyers to navigate the tax code, small businesses need simpler, more direct incentives to invest, hire, and expand. These policies were presented as a toolkit for the garage inventor, the local restaurant owner, the freelance consultant, and the ambitious startup founder. They address everything from the initial costs of launching a business to the complexities of research and development, all with the stated goal of making it easier to start, run, and grow a small enterprise in the United States.

One of the most significant new tools is what the bill's sponsors dubbed the "Start-Up and Scale-Up" deduction. This provision directly tackles two of the biggest financial hurdles for any new enterprise: the initial cost of getting off the ground and the subsequent cost of expansion. Under the old tax law, a new business could immediately deduct only a small portion of its start-up expenditures—things like market research, legal fees, and regulatory filings—up to a maximum of $5,000. Any costs beyond that had to be capitalized and amortized, meaning they were deducted in small increments over a lengthy 15-year period. This was a slow and often frustrating process for a cash-strapped new business.

The OBBB throws that old system out the window. It dramatically increases the amount of start-up costs that can be immediately deducted in the first year of operation. The new law allows a business to deduct up to $50,000 in qualified start-up and organizational costs. This tenfold increase means a new company can recover a much larger chunk of its initial investment right away, freeing up vital capital that can be used for inventory, marketing, or hiring its first employees. The deduction does begin to phase out for businesses with total start-up costs exceeding $250,000, a measure designed to ensure the primary benefit is targeted at truly small, nascent companies.

The second part of this provision, the "Scale-Up" deduction, is an entirely new concept in the tax code. It is designed for existing small businesses that are ready to grow. This new rule allows a qualifying small business—defined as one with average annual gross receipts of less than $5 million over the preceding three years—to immediately deduct up to $100,000 per year in specific "scaling investments." This category is intentionally broader than the traditional definition of capital expenditures. It includes intangible investments crucial for growth, such as developing new software systems, conducting extensive employee training programs, or launching major marketing and advertising campaigns.

This "Scale-Up" deduction is separate from and in addition to the 100% bonus depreciation for tangible property like machinery and equipment. The goal is to provide a powerful, immediate tax incentive for small businesses to invest not just in physical assets, but in the systems, skills, and market presence needed to reach the next level of success. Proponents argued that this would help level the playing field, allowing smaller, nimble companies to make the same kinds of strategic growth investments that larger corporations often take for granted, without the long wait for a tax benefit.

The OBBB also takes on one of an area of the tax code notoriously famous for its complexity: the Research and Development (R&D) tax credit. This credit has existed for decades to incentivize American innovation, but its intricate rules and documentation requirements often made it inaccessible to the very small businesses and startups that are engines of new ideas. Many small business owners simply lacked the accounting resources to navigate the four-part tests and complex calculations required to claim the credit. The OBBB attempts to remedy this with a major simplification and enhancement.

The key change is the creation of an optional "safe harbor" calculation specifically for small businesses. Instead of going through the traditional, labyrinthine process of calculating the credit, a qualifying small business can now elect to take a straightforward flat credit equal to 10% of its qualified research expenditures for the year. This simplifies the process immensely. A small tech firm that spends $200,000 on developing a new app no longer needs a costly study to document its R&D; it can simply elect to take a $20,000 tax credit. This provision is available to any business with less than $20 million in average annual gross receipts.

Beyond simplification, the bill significantly enhances the value of the R&D credit for the newest companies, particularly those that are not yet profitable. Before the OBBB, certain qualified startups could claim a portion of their R&D credit—up to $250,000—as a refund against their payroll taxes. This was a critical lifeline, as pre-profit companies have no income tax liability to offset, making traditional credits worthless to them. The OBBB doubles down on this concept. It doubles the maximum refundable amount from $250,000 to $500,000 per year.

Furthermore, it expands the definition of a "qualified small business" eligible for this payroll tax offset. The old rules limited it to companies that were less than five years old and had less than $5 million in gross receipts. The new law extends this, making the benefit available to companies up to seven years old and with gross receipts of up to $10 million. This change acknowledges the reality that for many high-tech or biotech startups, the path to profitability can take longer than five years. It provides a larger, more accessible pool of cash for innovative young companies to hire scientists, engineers, and developers.

Perhaps the most novel small business provision in the entire One Big Beautiful Bill is the creation of a brand-new type of tax-advantaged savings vehicle: the "Entrepreneurial Savings Account," or ESA. Modeled loosely on health savings accounts (HSAs) and retirement accounts, the ESA is designed to lower the financial barrier to starting a business by allowing individuals to save for their future venture with pre-tax dollars. The concept is a radical departure from previous policy, which generally only offered tax benefits after a business was already up and running.

Here is how the Entrepreneurial Savings Account works: any individual can contribute up to $10,000 per year of their pre-tax income into a designated ESA. This contribution is deductible from their taxable income, much like a traditional IRA contribution. The money in the account can then grow tax-deferred. The real magic happens when the money is withdrawn. If the account holder withdraws the funds to pay for "qualified business start-up expenses," the withdrawal is completely, 100% tax-free.

The list of qualified expenses is broad, covering the essentials of launching a new enterprise. It includes costs such as government filing fees, legal and consulting services, the purchase of initial equipment and inventory, rent for the first three months of a commercial lease, and initial marketing expenses. The goal is to create a dedicated, tax-free war chest that an aspiring entrepreneur can build up over several years before taking the leap.

To address the obvious question of what happens if someone saves in an ESA but never starts a business, the bill includes a flexible rollover provision. If, after a minimum of three years, the account holder decides not to pursue their business idea, they can roll the entire balance of their ESA directly into a traditional retirement account, such as a 401(k) or an IRA. At that point, the funds would simply become part of their retirement savings, subject to the normal rules and taxes upon withdrawal in their later years. This feature was designed to significantly lower the risk of saving for a business. The worst-case scenario is that you've simply ended up with more tax-deferred retirement savings.

During the congressional debates, proponents of the ESA hailed it as a revolutionary tool to democratize entrepreneurship. They argued that for too long, the ability to start a business has been tied to personal wealth or access to family money. The ESA, they claimed, gives anyone with a good idea and the discipline to save a clear, tax-advantaged path to accumulating the necessary seed capital. It was framed as a policy that rewards foresight and empowers individuals to build their own futures.

Critics, however, viewed the ESA with more skepticism. They argued it would primarily function as a new tax shelter for high-income individuals, who are both more likely to have the disposable income to contribute and more likely to start a business in the first place. Some tax policy experts warned that the definition of "qualified business start-up expenses" could be exploited, and that the program would be difficult for the IRS to police effectively. They also pointed to the cost in lost tax revenue, arguing that it was an expensive subsidy that might not result in a significant number of new business creations that wouldn't have happened anyway.

Finally, the OBBB addresses one of the most persistent complaints from small business owners: the ever-growing mountain of administrative and compliance burdens. The bill contains several provisions aimed at providing relief from paperwork and red tape. One of the most important of these is a further expansion of the eligibility to use the cash method of accounting. The TCJA had already raised the gross receipts threshold for this simpler accounting method to $25 million. The OBBB pushes that ceiling significantly higher, to $40 million.

This is a more impactful change than it might sound. The alternative, accrual accounting, requires businesses to recognize revenue when it is earned and expenses when they are incurred, regardless of when cash actually changes hands. This is a far more complex system that often requires professional accounting help. The cash method is much simpler: you recognize income when you get paid and expenses when you pay your bills. By raising the threshold to $40 million, the OBBB allows a much larger swath of small and medium-sized businesses to use this simpler, more intuitive method, saving them time and money on accounting fees.

In a similar vein, the bill enacts a temporary "regulatory pause" for small businesses. It places a five-year moratorium on the IRS's ability to implement most new information reporting requirements on businesses with fewer than 50 employees. This was a direct response to concerns from small business advocacy groups who felt they were being buried under an avalanche of new reporting rules, such as the controversial 1099-K reporting threshold changes for payment processors. Proponents of the moratorium argued that it would give "Main Street" a much-needed breathing spell, allowing them to focus on running their businesses instead of constantly adapting to new compliance regimes.

Of course, these simplification measures were not without their detractors. Opponents, including some former Treasury officials, argued that raising the cash accounting threshold too high could lead to a less accurate picture of a company's financial health and create opportunities for companies to manipulate their income for tax purposes. Similarly, they contended that the moratorium on new reporting requirements, while popular with business owners, could hamper the IRS's ability to enforce tax laws and close the "tax gap"—the difference between what is owed and what is actually paid. They argued that it sacrificed tax enforcement for the sake of administrative convenience.

Taken together, these various provisions—the Start-Up and Scale-Up deduction, the enhanced R&D credit, the new Entrepreneurial Savings Accounts, and the administrative relief measures—represent a multi-pronged strategy. They aim to make the tax code not just less costly for small businesses, but fundamentally more supportive of their life cycle, from conception and birth to growth and maturity. The success of this strategy will be measured in the years to come, not in the halls of Congress, but in the number of new storefronts that open, new products that are invented, and new jobs that are created across the country.

CHAPTER SIX: Changes to the Estate Tax: What It Means for Families

There are few taxes in the United States that generate as much heated debate, and as much confusion, as the federal estate tax. Known more colloquially—and often pejoratively—as the "death tax," it is a tax levied not on a person's income, but on the total value of their assets left behind for their heirs. It is a concept that touches upon fundamental American ideas about wealth, fairness, family, and legacy. For decades, the rules surrounding this tax have been a political football, with exemption levels and rates changing with the shifting winds in Washington. The One Big Beautiful Bill wades directly into this controversy, making some of the most significant and permanent changes to the estate tax in a generation.

To understand what the OBBB does, we must first understand the system it replaces. The estate tax is not a tax that affects most American families. The law has always allowed a certain amount of an estate's value, known as the "exemption amount," to be passed on to heirs completely free from federal tax. Only the value of the estate *above* this very high threshold is subject to the tax, which is levied at a top rate of 40%. The size of this exemption amount is the all-important number that determines whether a family needs to worry about the tax at all.

As we discussed in Chapter Two, the 2017 Tax Cuts and Jobs Act (TCJA) made a major, but temporary, change to this number. It effectively doubled the base exemption amount. Through annual adjustments for inflation, this exemption had grown from $5.49 million per person in 2017 to over $13.6 million by the beginning of 2025. This meant an individual could leave assets worth up to that amount to their heirs without triggering the tax. However, this was a temporary state of affairs. The TCJA's provision was set to expire at the end of 2025, at which point the exemption was scheduled to snap back to its pre-2018 level, which would have been around $7 million per person after inflation.

This looming deadline, often called the estate tax "cliff," created a tremendous amount of uncertainty for families, business owners, and farmers. Estate planning is a long-term endeavor, and the prospect of the exemption being suddenly cut in half made it nearly impossible to develop a stable, long-term strategy. The primary change the One Big Beautiful Bill makes to the estate tax is to march right up to this cliff and dismantle it entirely. The bill first repeals the sunset provision, preventing the exemption from being slashed. But it doesn't stop there.

The OBBB then takes the inflation-adjusted exemption amount from the TCJA and increases it further, establishing a new, permanent base exemption of $15 million per person. This new, higher exemption is also indexed for inflation, meaning the $15 million figure will continue to grow in the years ahead to keep pace with the rising cost of living. This change from a temporary, fluctuating policy to a permanent, high-exemption system is the cornerstone of the bill's estate tax reform. It provides a level of long-term certainty that has been absent from estate planning for many years.

To fully grasp the impact of this change, we must also consider the concept of "portability." Portability is a rule that allows a surviving spouse to use any unused portion of their deceased spouse's exemption. It effectively allows a married couple to combine their individual exemptions. With the new, permanent $15 million exemption, this means a married couple can now pass on a combined total of $30 million (plus all future inflation adjustments) to their heirs without paying a single penny in federal estate tax. This is a monumental shift that fundamentally alters the landscape for family wealth transfer in the United States.

While the OBBB makes a huge change to the estate tax itself, just as important is what it chose *not* to change. In the world of estate planning, there is a powerful but often misunderstood rule known as "stepped-up basis." This rule is a cornerstone of how inherited assets are treated for tax purposes, and the OBBB leaves it completely untouched. In simple terms, when you inherit an asset—like a portfolio of stocks, a piece of real estate, or a family business—its cost basis for tax purposes gets "stepped up" to its fair market value on the date of the original owner's death.

An example makes this clear. Let's say your mother bought 1,000 shares of a stock for $10 per share many years ago, for a total cost of $10,000. Over the decades, the stock performed spectacularly, and at the time of her passing, it is now worth $1,000 per share, making the portfolio worth $1 million. When you inherit that stock, the "stepped-up basis" rule means your cost basis is not the original $10,000; it is the current market value of $1 million. If you were to sell the entire portfolio the next day for $1 million, you would owe absolutely no federal capital gains tax. The $990,000 of growth the stock experienced during your mother's lifetime is never subject to capital gains tax.

For years, there have been proposals from various policymakers to eliminate or significantly limit this stepped-up basis rule. The argument was that it functions as a massive, untaxed loophole for the heirs of wealthy individuals. The OBBB considered and explicitly rejected these proposals. By preserving the stepped-up basis rule while simultaneously raising the estate tax exemption to $15 million per person, the bill delivers a powerful one-two punch of tax relief for the transfer of generational wealth. Heirs will not only be exempt from the estate tax on up to $30 million per couple, but they will also be able to sell those inherited assets without paying capital gains tax on decades of appreciation.

The primary argument made by the proponents of these changes centered on the preservation of family farms and businesses. This has long been the most emotionally resonant and politically effective case for raising the estate tax exemption. The scenario painted by supporters is a common one: a family has spent generations building a farm or a local business. The value of their land, buildings, and equipment might be quite high on paper—perhaps $12 million—but the family itself is often "asset-rich and cash-poor." They do not have millions of dollars sitting in a bank account to pay a potential tax bill.

The fear was that a low estate tax exemption would present the next generation with a devastating choice: sell off large portions of the farm or even the entire family business simply to raise the cash needed to pay the IRS. This, proponents argued, was not just a tax issue but a threat to the fabric of rural communities and Main Street economies. They contended that the estate tax was actively destroying the very multi-generational enterprises it should be encouraging.

From this perspective, the OBBB's increase of the exemption to $15 million per person ($30 million per couple) is presented as the ultimate shield for these families. The new, much higher threshold ensures that the vast, overwhelming majority of family farms and businesses in the country will be passed down to the next generation without the looming threat of a federal estate tax bill. This provides peace of mind and allows these families to focus on continuing their legacy rather than on liquidating it.

Of course, these dramatic changes to the estate tax were among the most contentious provisions in the entire One Big Beautiful Bill. Opponents raised several fundamental objections, arguing that the bill's approach would have damaging long-term consequences for the country's social and fiscal health. The most prominent criticism is that gutting the estate tax will dramatically accelerate the concentration of wealth in the hands of a few powerful families.

Critics argue that the estate tax, even if it only affects a tiny fraction of the population, serves a vital societal function. They see it as a check on the formation of a permanent financial aristocracy, ensuring that, over generations, vast fortunes are put back into circulation for public use rather than being endlessly consolidated. From this viewpoint, raising the exemption to such a high level is a fiscally reckless move that exacerbates wealth inequality, making it harder for those without inherited wealth to move up the economic ladder.

The fiscal impact was another major point of contention. While the number of estates subject to the tax is small, the amounts collected from those few estates can be substantial. Analysis cited by opponents during the congressional debate projected that making the higher exemption permanent and increasing it further would reduce federal revenues by hundreds of billions of dollars over the next decade. This lost revenue, they argued, would either add directly to the national debt, placing a greater burden on future generations, or necessitate deeper cuts to vital public programs.

Furthermore, critics repeatedly pointed to statistics showing just how few Americans are actually affected by the estate tax. Under the TCJA's already high exemption levels, fewer than 2,000 estates in the entire country were expected to owe any federal estate tax in a given year, a figure representing less than 0.1% of all deaths. By increasing the exemption to $15 million per person, the OBBB shrinks that number even further. Opponents framed this not as a broad-based tax cut, but as a massive giveaway targeted at the absolute wealthiest 0.1%, with its costs distributed across the entire population.

To understand the full scope of the OBBB's changes, one must also look at a related, and even more technical, area of tax law: the Generation-Skipping Transfer (GST) tax. This is a separate, parallel tax designed for a very specific purpose: to prevent the wealthiest families from using a simple loophole to avoid estate taxes for a generation. Without this tax, a very wealthy grandparent could leave their fortune directly to their grandchildren, "skipping" the generation of their children entirely. That way, the assets would only be subject to the estate tax once (when the grandchild dies) instead of twice (once when the child dies, and again when the grandchild dies).

To close this loophole, the tax code imposes the GST tax on such transfers. Crucially, the GST tax has its own exemption amount, and for the sake of simplicity and consistency, Congress has historically tied the GST tax exemption directly to the estate tax exemption. The One Big Beautiful Bill continues this long-standing tradition. By raising the estate tax exemption to $15 million, the bill automatically raises the GST tax exemption to $15 million as well.

This is a critical detail for dynastic wealth planning. It means that a wealthy individual can not only leave up to $15 million to their children tax-free, but they can also place up to $15 million into a long-term trust for their grandchildren or even great-grandchildren without triggering this additional layer of tax. A married couple can combine their GST exemptions to shield $30 million in this manner. This provision ensures that the benefits of the higher estate tax exemption can be projected deep into the future, allowing for the creation of "dynasty trusts" that can preserve family wealth for many generations to come.

So, what do all these changes mean for the average family's financial planning? The most immediate consequence is a dramatic simplification for a huge number of people. With a new federal exemption of $30 million for a married couple, the vast majority of Americans—even many who are quite affluent—can now confidently say that the federal estate tax is not something they will ever have to worry about. For decades, a primary goal of estate planning for many successful professionals and small business owners was minimizing this potential tax. That concern has now been effectively eliminated for all but the wealthiest households.

This shifts the focus of estate planning significantly. Instead of complex strategies aimed at reducing the size of a taxable estate, the main goals for most families will now revolve around other, more practical matters. These include ensuring a smooth and orderly transfer of assets, protecting heirs from making poor financial decisions, and planning for potential incapacity. The preservation of the "stepped-up basis" rule also means that minimizing capital gains taxes for heirs will remain a paramount goal.

It is also vital to remember that the OBBB only changes the *federal* estate tax. As of 2025, a number of states still levy their own, separate estate or inheritance taxes, and they often have much lower exemption amounts than the federal government. For residents of states like New York, Illinois, Massachusetts, or Oregon, state-level estate tax planning remains a very real and important concern. The OBBB does nothing to change these state laws, creating a situation where a family could have an estate valued at, for example, $8 million, owe no federal tax, but still be faced with a significant state tax bill.

For the ultra-wealthy—those with estates that still exceed the new, very high $30 million-per-couple threshold—the complicated world of advanced estate tax planning will certainly continue. The use of sophisticated trusts and gifting strategies will not disappear. However, the goalposts have been moved so dramatically that the planning calculus has changed for everyone. The OBBB has effectively transformed the federal estate tax from a concern for the merely wealthy into a tax that is exclusively reserved for the ultra-rich.

CHAPTER SEVEN: The Future of the State and Local Tax (SALT) Deduction

Few provisions in the vast American tax code have generated as much raw political emotion, regional animosity, and sheer legislative drama as the deduction for state and local taxes, universally known by its four-letter acronym: SALT. For over a century, this deduction was a quiet, unassuming feature of the federal system, allowing taxpayers to subtract the taxes they paid to their state and local governments from the income they reported to the federal government. Then, in 2017, the Tax Cuts and Jobs Act transformed it from a technical provision into a political firestorm by slapping a $10,000 cap on it. The One Big Beautiful Bill does not extinguish this fire, but it does turn down the heat considerably, offering a significant, if temporary, truce in the ongoing SALT wars.

To understand the change, you must first appreciate the system it modifies. Before the TCJA, if you itemized your deductions (as opposed to taking the standard deduction), you could deduct the full amount of your state and local property taxes, plus either your state income taxes or your state sales taxes, whichever was greater. For residents of states with high property values and high income tax rates—think New York, New Jersey, California, Connecticut, and Illinois—this was an incredibly valuable tax break. A homeowner in a New York City suburb might pay $25,000 in property taxes and another $20,000 in state income taxes. Before 2018, they could deduct that entire $45,000, reducing their federally taxable income by that amount.

The TCJA brought this to an abrupt halt. It declared that, no matter how much you paid in state and local taxes, you could only deduct a maximum of $10,000 per household. This cap applied to everyone—both single individuals and married couples filing jointly. Overnight, our hypothetical New York family saw their SALT deduction plummet from a potential $45,000 to just $10,000. This was, for many, the single most painful part of the

2017 tax law, a massive tax increase that offset many of the other benefits of the TCJA for residents of these high-tax states.

The political fallout was immediate and intense. Lawmakers from the affected states, primarily Democrats but also a significant number of Republicans, cried foul. They argued that the cap was an unfair double tax, forcing their constituents to pay federal income tax on the money they had already paid to their state and local governments. They also charged that the cap was a politically targeted attack, as the states most harmed by it were predominantly "blue" states that had not supported the administration in power. For the next eight years, the "SALT caucus" in Congress, a bipartisan coalition from these states, fought relentlessly to repeal the cap, making it a constant sticking point in nearly every major fiscal negotiation.

The One Big Beautiful Bill offers a carefully crafted compromise, a political solution designed to win over just enough of these SALT-focused lawmakers to get the larger bill across the finish line. The OBBB does not fully repeal the $10,000 cap. Instead, it temporarily and dramatically raises it. For a period of five years, starting with the 2026 tax year, the cap on the state and local tax deduction is increased from $10,000 to $40,000. This is a fourfold increase, a change that will provide immediate and substantial tax relief to millions of households.

However, the bill's authors added two very important pieces of fine print to this SALT relief. First, the new, higher cap is subject to an income limitation. The full $40,000 deduction is only available to individuals with a modified adjusted gross income of up to $500,000, or married couples filing jointly with an income of up to $1 million. For taxpayers with incomes above these thresholds, the cap is gradually phased down. This was a key concession to fiscal conservatives, allowing proponents to argue that the relief is targeted at the middle and upper-middle class, not just a giveaway to the wealthiest taxpayers in the highest-tax states.

Second, the new $40,000 cap, like the old $10,000 cap, still applies to the household as a whole. It is not doubled for married couples. A single person with an income of $450,000 can deduct up to $40,000 in SALT. A married couple with a combined income of $900,000 can also deduct up to $40,000. This preserves what critics call a "marriage penalty." For two high-earning individuals in a high-tax state, their combined SALT deduction could be much higher if they remained unmarried than if they were to file a joint return. While the higher cap makes this penalty less severe than the old $10,000 limit, it remains a feature of the law.

The most crucial detail of all is the provision's temporary nature. The new $40,000 cap is only in effect for five tax years: 2026, 2027, 2028, 2029, and 2030. On January 1, 2031, unless a future Congress acts to extend it, the cap is scheduled to revert to its original $10,000 level (which would then be indexed for inflation from that point forward). This legislative tactic, using a temporary "patch" to solve a political problem, is common in Washington. It allowed the bill's sponsors to reduce the official ten-year cost of the provision, making the overall bill appear more fiscally responsible on paper.

The practical impact of this change will be felt most acutely in the suburbs and cities of coastal states. Let's return to our family in New Jersey paying $25,000 in property taxes and $15,000 in state income taxes, for a total of $40,000 in SALT payments. For the past eight years, their deduction was capped at $10,000. Now, assuming their income is below the new threshold, they will be able to deduct the full $40,000. For a family in the 24% tax bracket, this additional $30,000 deduction translates into a federal tax cut of $7,200 per year. This is a significant amount of money that will flow directly back into the pockets of households that have been feeling the pinch of the cap.

The political calculus behind this compromise was delicate and essential to the OBBB's passage. Full repeal of the SALT cap was a non-starter for the majority of lawmakers from low-tax states like Florida, Texas, and Tennessee. They have long argued that the SALT deduction is a federal subsidy for high-spending state governments. From their perspective, a Texan who pays no state income tax should not have to indirectly subsidize the high-tax, high-service model of California through the federal tax code. They see the cap as a way to level the playing field between the states.

By offering a temporary, income-limited increase rather than a full repeal, the OBBB's leadership found a tenable middle ground. The "blue state" lawmakers could declare a major victory for their constituents, having secured tax relief that was four times greater than the old cap. This was enough for a critical number of them to vote "yes" on the entire OBBB package, even if they had reservations about other parts of the bill. At the same time, the "red state" lawmakers could argue that they held the line against a full repeal, limited the benefit to those not in the highest income brackets, and ensured the change was not permanent, thereby limiting the long-term cost to the Treasury.

The arguments in favor of this change focus on fairness and economic common sense. Proponents contend that the $10,000 cap was an arbitrary and punitive measure that distorted the tax code and unfairly burdened millions of families. They argue that income that is taken by one level of government should not be considered fair game for taxation by another. Raising the cap, in their view, is simply a partial restoration of a century-old principle of tax law. They also argue that the high cost of living in states like California and New York means that even families with seemingly high incomes are often struggling with household budgets, and this tax relief is desperately needed.

On the other side of the debate, critics argue that raising the SALT cap, even temporarily, is a step in the wrong direction. They point to analyses from non-partisan groups like the Tax Policy Center and the Committee for a Responsible Federal Budget, which consistently show that the benefits of SALT deductions flow overwhelmingly to high-income households. Even with an income limit of $1 million for the new cap, the vast majority of the tax relief will go to households in the top 20% of the income distribution, simply because they are the ones who are most likely to itemize their deductions and have state and local tax bills that exceed $10,000.

Opponents label the provision as a fiscally irresponsible giveaway to the wealthy. They argue that the hundreds of billions of dollars in lost tax revenue over the next decade would be better spent on programs that benefit a broader segment of the population or on reducing the national debt. They also maintain the philosophical argument that the federal government should not be in the business of subsidizing the policy choices of high-tax state governments. If a state chooses to levy high taxes to pay for extensive public services, that is a decision for the residents of that state, and its cost should not be offset by federal taxpayers across the country.

The temporary nature of the fix is another major source of criticism. Opponents see it as a classic Washington budget gimmick. By making the provision expire after five years, the official "score" of the bill from the Congressional Budget Office looks much smaller. However, everyone in Washington knows that when a popular tax break is set to expire, there will be immense political pressure to extend it. Critics argue that this creates a dishonest picture of the bill's true long-term fiscal impact and simply sets up another "fiscal cliff" and another political battle a few years down the road.

This change could also have a ripple effect on the fiscal policies of state governments themselves. One of the stated goals of the original $10,000 cap was to put political pressure on high-tax states to lower their tax burdens. With their residents no longer able to fully deduct those taxes, the theory went, they would be more likely to demand tax cuts at the state level. The evidence of whether this has actually worked is mixed, but raising the cap to $40,000 certainly removes a significant amount of that pressure. State lawmakers may now feel they have more leeway to maintain or even increase state taxes, knowing that a larger portion of that cost will be softened by a federal deduction for their residents.

For individual taxpayers and their financial advisors, the new rule introduces a new layer of planning considerations. For the next five years, many more people in high-tax states will find it beneficial to itemize their deductions rather than taking the standard deduction. This may change the math on decisions like whether to prepay property taxes before the end of the year. The five-year horizon also creates a planning challenge. Do you make financial decisions based on the assumption that the $40,000 cap will be extended, or do you plan for the possibility that it will snap back to the much lower $10,000 level in 2031?

This uncertainty is now a baked-in feature of the tax code. The OBBB did not solve the SALT problem; it simply bought five years of political peace. The fundamental disagreement over whether the SALT deduction is a fair reflection of a taxpayer's ability to pay or a wasteful subsidy for wealthy states remains as potent as ever. The bill has reshaped the battlefield, but the war over SALT is far from over. It is merely in a temporary ceasefire, with both sides already preparing their arguments for the next major confrontation.

CHAPTER EIGHT: Reforming SNAP: New Work Requirements and Eligibility

The Supplemental Nutrition Assistance Program, or SNAP, is one of the most widely known and frequently debated components of the American social safety net. For millions of families, it is the program that helps put food on the table when times are tough. Formerly known as the Food Stamp Program, SNAP provides a monthly benefit, loaded onto an Electronic Benefit Transfer (EBT) card, that can be used to purchase groceries. Given its size and its direct connection to the fundamental need for food, it has long been a focal point for policymakers seeking to reform federal welfare programs. The One Big Beautiful Bill makes some of the most profound changes to SNAP in decades, fundamentally reshaping who is eligible for benefits and what they must do to receive them.

At the heart of the OBBB's reforms is a significant expansion of work requirements. The idea of tying public assistance to work is not new to SNAP. For years, a rule has existed for a specific group known as "Able-Bodied Adults Without Dependents," or ABAWDs. These are individuals between the ages of 18 and 49 who are not disabled and do not have minor children living in their home. Under the old system, these ABAWDs could only receive SNAP benefits for three months in a three-year period unless they were working or participating in a work-training program for at least 20 hours per week. The OBBB takes this existing framework and applies it more broadly and more strictly than ever before.

The first major change is an expansion of the age range for individuals considered ABAWDs. The bill raises the maximum age for these work requirements from 49 up to 62. This means that a 58-year-old individual with no dependents, who previously would have been exempt from the three-month time limit based on their age, is now subject to the same strict work rules. They must now document work or training hours to receive food assistance for more than a brief period. This single change brings a large cohort of older, low-income Americans under the umbrella of the work requirement rules for the very first time.

Perhaps the most dramatic shift, however, is the creation of an entirely new work requirement for parents of school-aged children. Historically, parents with dependent children under the age of 18 were exempt from the ABAWD time limits. The OBBB changes this long-standing policy. Under the new law, a parent or caretaker relative is now required to meet a work requirement if their youngest child is over the age of six. The bill sets this new requirement at 30 hours per week of work, participation in a state-approved job training program, or a combination of the two.

This is a monumental change to the structure of the program. Consider a single mother with an eight-year-old child. Previously, she would have been eligible for SNAP based on her household income, without a federal work mandate. Now, she must find a way to document 30 hours of work or training activity each week. If she is unable to do so, her entire household—including her child—could lose its SNAP benefits. The work requirement is tied to the parent's compliance, but the consequence of non-compliance is felt by the entire family.

The OBBB is very specific about what constitutes "work" for the purposes of meeting these new requirements. For both the expanded ABAWD group and for parents, acceptable activities include paid employment (including self-employment), on-the-job training, and participation in specific state-run or federally approved workforce development programs. The bill notably places stricter limits on what can be counted as a qualifying activity. For example, it narrows the definition of acceptable job training programs and puts a cap on the number of hours that can be fulfilled through volunteer work or "workfare," where an individual works for a public or non-profit entity in exchange for their benefits.

The consequences for failing to meet these new, stricter standards are severe. For an ABAWD, the rule remains a hard time limit: three months of benefits, and then they are cut off until they can document compliance or until the three-year period resets. For a parent who fails to meet the 30-hour weekly requirement, the penalty is a graduated sanction. The first instance of non-compliance results in a loss of benefits for three months. A second instance results in a six-month disqualification. A third instance leads to a permanent disqualification from the program for that parent, effectively ending benefits for the household unless another adult can meet the requirements.

Beyond imposing new work rules, the One Big Beautiful Bill also tightens the financial eligibility criteria for the program. One of the most significant changes in this area is the elimination of a policy option known as "Broad-Based Categorical Eligibility," or BBCE. This is a technical-sounding term for a very important piece of administrative flexibility that was used by the majority of states. In simple terms, BBCE allowed states to make a household automatically eligible for SNAP if they were already receiving a benefit from another program, like Temporary Assistance for Needy Families (TANF).

This was important because many states used their TANF programs to provide non-cash benefits, like a childcare voucher or an informational pamphlet, and these programs often had more lenient asset tests than the federal SNAP rules. The federal rules generally limit a household to about $2,750 in countable assets (or slightly more for households with an elderly or disabled member). BBCE allowed states to effectively bypass this federal asset test for many applicants. A family might have $5,000 in a savings account—perhaps set aside for a new car to get to work—which would make them ineligible under the federal rules, but they could still qualify for SNAP through BBCE in many states.

The OBBB abolishes the BBCE option entirely. It establishes a uniform, national standard for asset limits. Every household applying for SNAP in every state must now meet the federal asset test. There are no more state-level waivers or workarounds. This means that families with even modest savings could now find themselves ineligible for food assistance. The bill's authors argued this was a matter of fairness and program integrity, ensuring that benefits are targeted only to those with the most limited resources. Critics, however, argue that this change penalizes families for responsible saving and could force them to drain their emergency funds before they can qualify for help.

Another area where the OBBB curtails state flexibility is in the use of waivers for the ABAWD work requirements. Under the old system, states could request a waiver from the three-month time limit for specific geographic areas that had high unemployment rates or a demonstrable lack of sufficient jobs. This was a recognition that it might be unreasonable to expect someone to find work in a depressed local economy. These waivers were common, and at various times, large portions of many states were covered by them, effectively suspending the work requirement time clock in those areas.

The One Big Beautiful Bill severely restricts this waiver authority. The new law raises the threshold for what qualifies as a high-unemployment area, making it much more difficult for any county or region to be granted a waiver. It also places a hard cap on the percentage of a state's population that can be covered by a waiver at any one time. The clear intent and effect of this provision is to make the ABAWD work requirements a nearly universal, nationwide mandate with very few exceptions. The local economic conditions of a specific town or county are no longer a primary factor in whether its residents are subject to the time limit.

The public debate over these sweeping reforms to SNAP was one of the most ideologically charged of the entire OBBB legislative battle. Proponents of the changes framed them as essential "pro-work" reforms designed to restore the program to its original purpose as a temporary safety net. They argued that the previous system encouraged dependency on government assistance and created a disincentive for individuals to enter or remain in the workforce. The central theme of their argument was the "dignity of work" and the belief that employment is the surest and most effective path out of poverty.

Supporters contended that the new, stricter work requirements would not only save taxpayer money by reducing the number of people on the program, but that they would also benefit the recipients themselves by pushing them toward self-sufficiency. They pointed to the strong economy and low national unemployment rate as evidence that jobs were available for those willing to work. The message was that able-bodied adults, including parents of older children, should be expected to work or prepare for work in exchange for receiving public benefits. The tightening of asset tests was similarly defended as a common-sense measure to ensure that taxpayer-funded food assistance is reserved for the truly needy.

On the other side of the aisle, opponents of these changes painted a starkly different picture. They argued that the new rules were cruel and would lead to a significant increase in hunger and hardship for millions of Americans, including children. They contended that the reforms are based on a fundamental misunderstanding of the lives of the poor and the nature of the low-wage job market. Many SNAP recipients who are not working, they argued, face significant and often invisible barriers to employment, such as chronic health conditions, a lack of affordable childcare, unreliable transportation, or living in an area with few job opportunities.

Critics pointed to numerous studies of existing work requirements that suggested they often fail to lift people out of poverty. Instead, these studies found that the primary effect of such rules is simply that large numbers of people lose their benefits, not that they find stable, well-paying jobs. The administrative burden of tracking and documenting work hours, they argued, is a setup for failure for many individuals who may be struggling with housing instability or chaotic work schedules in the gig economy. For a low-wage worker whose hours fluctuate from week to week, meeting a rigid 30-hour mandate could be nearly impossible.

The new work requirement for parents was a particular flashpoint for opposition. Critics argued that this policy ignores the immense value of the caregiving work that parents do and fails to account for the high cost and limited availability of quality childcare, especially for parents who might have to work non-traditional hours. They warned that sanctioning an entire family because a parent is unable to meet the work requirement would have devastating long-term consequences for the health and development of children. The elimination of state flexibility through waivers and BBCE was also heavily criticized as a one-size-fits-all federal mandate that ignores the diverse economic realities of different states and communities.

From a practical standpoint, the implementation of these reforms represents a massive undertaking for state agencies that administer the SNAP program. They must now develop and deploy complex new systems to track the work activities of a much larger portion of their caseload. This involves verifying employment, monitoring hours worked, approving training programs, and processing sanctions for non-compliance. It requires a significant increase in staffing and resources for functions that are notoriously difficult and time-consuming.

For individuals applying for or seeking to maintain their SNAP benefits, the process will become significantly more complex. Applicants will face a much greater documentation burden. A 55-year-old man will now need to provide pay stubs or letters from employers to prove he is working. A mother of two will need to submit paperwork from her job training program to show she is meeting the 30-hour weekly mandate. A single mistake, a lost document, or a missed deadline could result in the loss of a family's food assistance. The OBBB has transformed SNAP from a program primarily focused on income eligibility into one that is now heavily focused on monitoring and enforcing work.

CHAPTER NINE: The Overhaul of Medicaid: What You Need to Know

If the changes to SNAP described in the previous chapter represent a significant redesign of the nutritional safety net, the One Big Beautiful Bill's reforms to Medicaid are a wholesale demolition and reconstruction of the nation's healthcare safety net. Medicaid, the sprawling joint federal-state program that provides health coverage to over eighty million low-income Americans, is not merely being tweaked or adjusted. It is being fundamentally re-engineered from its financial foundations to its eligibility requirements. The OBBB's provisions replace a sixty-year-old financing agreement between Washington and the states with a completely new system, introduce nationwide work mandates, and effectively dismantle the Medicaid expansion that was a cornerstone of the Affordable Care Act (ACA).

To understand the magnitude of this overhaul, one must first understand the old system's financial architecture. Since its inception in 1965, Medicaid has operated on a matching-grant basis. For every dollar a state spent on its Medicaid program, the federal government would pay a percentage, known as the Federal Medical Assistance Percentage, or FMAP. This percentage varied from state to state based on per capita income, but the promise was always the same: for approved expenditures, the federal government's contribution was open-ended. If a state faced a recession, a natural disaster, or a public health crisis that caused enrollment to spike, federal funding would automatically increase to meet the new demand. This system made the federal government a full partner in the risks and costs of the program.

The One Big Beautiful Bill completely severs this open-ended commitment. It ends the FMAP system as it has existed for decades and gives states a choice between two new, fundamentally different funding models: a block grant or a per-capita cap. While seemingly technical, this is the most consequential change to the program in its history. Under the block grant model, the federal government will provide each state with a single, fixed, lump-sum payment each year to run its entire Medicaid program. The initial amount of this grant is based on the state's Medicaid spending in a designated base year, trended forward with a specific inflation index. After that, the state is on its own. If enrollment surges or healthcare costs skyrocket beyond the inflation adjuster, the state must cover 100% of the additional costs itself.

The alternative model offered is the per-capita cap. Instead of one giant lump sum, the federal government provides a fixed amount of funding per enrollee. This funding is broken down by different categories of beneficiaries—for example, a state might receive one funding amount per elderly enrollee, a different amount per child, and another amount per disabled adult. This approach provides some protection against a sudden surge in enrollment—if more people qualify, the state receives more capped payments—but it still exposes the state to all the risk of rising healthcare costs *per person*. If a new, expensive drug comes to market or hospital costs in the state rise sharply, the federal per-person payment does not change. The state absorbs the full financial blow.

The proponents of this historic shift in funding argued that it was an essential move to control runaway federal spending and inject fiscal discipline into the Medicaid program. They contended that the old open-ended matching system created a perverse incentive for states to spend more, knowing that the federal government would always pick up a large portion of the tab. This, they claimed, led to bloated, inefficient programs with little accountability. The promise of the new block grant and per-capita cap systems is predictability for the federal budget. No longer an uncapped entitlement, Medicaid's cost to the federal taxpayer will now be a known, manageable line item.

The second major selling point for this new model was the promise of unprecedented state flexibility. The architects of the OBBB argued that in exchange for taking on more financial risk, states should be freed from the thicket of federal regulations that have long dictated how they must run their Medicaid programs. The bill grants states that adopt one of the new funding models sweeping new authority to design their programs as they see fit. This flexibility touches every aspect of the program, from who is covered to what services are provided.

Under the old rules, states were required to cover a list of "mandatory benefits," including things like hospital services, doctor visits, and nursing home care. The OBBB largely scraps this federal floor. States operating under a block grant will now have the authority to define their own benefit packages. A state could choose to offer a leaner plan that does not cover certain services, like dental or vision care, or it could require patients to pay more out-of-pocket for them. This flexibility allows states to tailor their programs to the specific needs of their populations and their own state budgets.

This new authority also extends to cost-sharing. Previously, federal law strictly limited the premiums and co-payments that states could charge to Medicaid recipients, recognizing that even small out-of-pocket costs can be a major barrier to care for low-income families. The OBBB removes many of these federal guardrails. States will now be permitted to implement higher premiums, create deductibles, and increase co-payments for doctor visits or prescription drugs. This is based on the principle of personal responsibility, with proponents arguing that requiring beneficiaries to have some "skin in the game" will encourage them to be more cost-conscious consumers of healthcare.

The combination of fixed federal funding and enhanced state flexibility is designed to transform Medicaid from a one-size-fits-all federal program into a collection of fifty distinct, state-run experiments. Proponents hailed this as a victory for federalism and innovation. They envisioned a future where states could act as "laboratories of democracy," developing new, market-based approaches to providing healthcare for the poor, free from the dictates of Washington bureaucrats. If one state designed a particularly effective and efficient program, others could choose to adopt its model.

Alongside this financial restructuring, the One Big Beautiful Bill imposes a nationwide work requirement for Medicaid eligibility, mirroring the reforms made to the SNAP program. Historically, the idea of tying health coverage to work status was highly controversial and was only implemented in a handful of states through temporary and heavily litigated federal waivers. The OBBB bypasses the waiver process and makes work a core, permanent condition of eligibility for a large segment of the population.

The new federal mandate applies to all able-bodied adult beneficiaries under the age of 65 who are not pregnant and are not the primary caregiver for a dependent child under the age of six. To remain eligible for Medicaid, these individuals must document at least 80 hours per month of engagement in "work activities." This can include employment, job searching, skills training, or community service. The bill does include exemptions for individuals who are medically certified as physically or mentally unfit for employment or those participating in a drug addiction treatment program.

The penalties for non-compliance are stark. The first time an individual fails to meet the 80-hour monthly requirement, their Medicaid coverage is suspended for three months. A second failure results in a six-month lockout. A third failure to comply can lead to a permanent disqualification from the program. Proponents of this policy argued that it is a common-sense measure to ensure that Medicaid serves as a temporary support system rather than a permanent way of life. They contended that it would encourage self-sufficiency and move more people from public assistance into the workforce, which they see as the most effective long-term solution to poverty and poor health.

The administrative challenge of this new requirement is immense. State Medicaid agencies, already stretched thin, must now build and manage a massive new bureaucracy dedicated to tracking and verifying the work activities of millions of people. This involves processing paperwork from employers, training programs, and volunteer organizations, as well as developing a system for adjudicating exemption requests and appeals. It is a complex and costly undertaking that fundamentally shifts the focus of state agencies from processing healthcare claims to monitoring beneficiary behavior.

The final, and perhaps most politically charged, element of the Medicaid overhaul is its impact on the expansion created by the Affordable Care Act. The ACA gave states the option to expand their Medicaid programs to cover nearly all adults with incomes up to 138% of the federal poverty level. To encourage states to do this, the federal government offered a special, enhanced matching rate, agreeing to pay for 90% of the costs for this newly eligible population, a much higher share than for traditional Medicaid enrollees. The OBBB effectively terminates this arrangement.

Under the new block grant or per-capita cap systems, the special 90% enhanced match for the expansion population is eliminated. The funding for these individuals is simply rolled into the state's overall fixed federal payment, calculated using the much lower, traditional matching rate. This completely rewrites the financial equation for the nearly three-dozen states that had adopted the expansion. What was once a fiscally attractive deal, with the federal government bearing most of the cost, suddenly becomes a massive potential liability for state budgets.

The practical effect of this change is to create an enormous incentive for states to roll back their Medicaid expansions. Faced with a fixed federal payment, states will have to decide if they can afford to continue covering the expansion population when every dollar spent on them is now a dollar that cannot be spent on the traditional Medicaid populations of children, pregnant women, seniors, or the disabled. Many policy experts predict this will lead a majority of expansion states to lower their income eligibility limits back down to their pre-ACA levels, a move that would cause millions of low-income working adults to lose their health coverage.

The opponents of the OBBB's Medicaid overhaul mounted a fierce resistance, arguing that the combination of these changes would have catastrophic consequences for both vulnerable families and the nation's healthcare system as a whole. They argued that "flexibility" and "innovation" are simply euphemisms for deep, unavoidable cuts. The core of their argument focused on the flawed nature of a fixed funding stream for healthcare. Unlike education or transportation, healthcare needs are unpredictable and can spike without warning. A new pandemic, the arrival of a transformative but expensive new treatment, or a local recession could cause a state's costs to soar far beyond what a block grant, even one indexed for inflation, could cover.

Critics warned that this would force states into an impossible position, forcing them to make draconian cuts year after year. These cuts would inevitably take the form of throwing people off the program, slashing benefits, and cutting payments to doctors and hospitals. This could trigger a "race to the bottom," as states, now in full competition with each other for limited resources, design ever-leaner programs to stay within their fixed budgets. The result, opponents claimed, would not be innovation, but a steady degradation of health coverage for the poor across the country.

The loss of the system's counter-cyclical nature was another major point of criticism. In an economic downturn, Medicaid has always served as an automatic stabilizer. As people lose their jobs and their employer-sponsored health insurance, they can turn to Medicaid for coverage, and federal funds automatically flow to states to help them shoulder the load. Under a block grant system, this automatic stabilizer is gone. A state facing a recession would see its Medicaid rolls swell at the very same moment its own tax revenues are plummeting, all while its federal health funding remains flat. This could turn a state-level recession into a full-blown fiscal and healthcare crisis.

The work requirements also drew heavy fire. Opponents argued that they are based on the false premise that most non-working Medicaid recipients are unemployed by choice. They pointed to data showing that the majority of adults on Medicaid who can work already are working, often in low-wage jobs with unstable or fluctuating hours that would make it incredibly difficult to consistently document 80 hours a month. For those who aren't working, it is often due to significant barriers like a personal health problem that doesn't rise to the level of a federal disability determination, a lack of affordable transportation, or the need to provide care for a sick family member.

Critics warned that the primary result of the work requirement would not be a surge in employment, but a surge in the number of people losing their health insurance due to red tape and bureaucracy. A lost pay stub, a missed deadline, or a simple paperwork error could result in a person with a chronic condition like diabetes or hypertension losing access to the care they need to manage their illness and stay healthy enough to work. This, they argued, is both cruel and counterproductive, as it would lead to people showing up in emergency rooms with more advanced, and far more expensive, health problems.

Finally, the critics decried the rollback of the ACA Medicaid expansion as a massive step backward for public health. They pointed to years of studies showing that states that expanded Medicaid saw improvements in health outcomes, reductions in premature deaths, and significant gains in financial security for low-income families. Forcing states to end this coverage, they argued, would erase these gains and lead to a dramatic increase in the number of uninsured Americans. This, in turn, would place immense strain on the entire healthcare system, particularly rural and safety-net hospitals, which rely heavily on Medicaid payments to keep their doors open. A surge in uncompensated care for the newly uninsured could be the final nail in the coffin for many of these struggling facilities.

CHAPTER TEN: A Massive Boost for National Defense and the Military

Where the One Big Beautiful Bill sought to shrink the federal government's role in social welfare programs, it performed a dramatic and expensive reversal when it came to national defense. The legislation authorizes a surge in military spending on a scale not seen in decades, reflecting a core tenet of the bill's philosophy: that a powerful, technologically superior military is the primary guarantor of American security and global influence. This chapter will explore the sheer size of this new investment and detail where the hundreds of billions of new dollars are intended to go, from buying the weapons of today to inventing the weapons of tomorrow.

The OBBB sets the top-line budget for the Department of Defense at a staggering $1.1 trillion for the coming fiscal year. This figure represents a nearly twenty percent increase over the previously enacted budget, an enormous year-over-year jump in peacetime. The bill's text makes it clear that this is not intended as a temporary surge, but as the establishment of a new, higher baseline for defense appropriations for the next decade. This commitment of resources elevates defense spending to a level of priority on par with the bill's sweeping tax cuts, fundamentally reordering the nation's fiscal landscape.

The stated rationale behind this massive reinvestment, repeated frequently by the bill's sponsors during the congressional debates, was the need to confront a world they described as more dangerous and competitive than at any time since the end of the Cold War. The bill's preamble specifically cites the rapid modernization of China's People's Liberation Army, the continued aggression of Russia, and persistent threats from nations like Iran and North Korea as justification for a renewed focus on "peace through strength." The argument was that years of budget caps and competing priorities had left the U.S. military worn down and at risk of losing its technological and numerical superiority over these "peer and near-peer adversaries."

A massive portion of the new funding is allocated to procurement, which is simply the process of buying new military hardware. The OBBB effectively gives the Pentagon a multi-billion-dollar shopping list to fill, with the goal of expanding and upgrading the arsenal of every branch of the armed forces. The bill is not just about buying more of the same; it is about accelerating the transition to the next generation of military technology across the board.

For the U.S. Air Force, the bill provides a major cash infusion to ramp up production of its most advanced aircraft. Funding is significantly increased for the F-35 Lightning II, the versatile stealth fighter that forms the backbone of modern air power. More critically, the OBBB injects billions into the highly classified Next Generation Air Dominance (NGAD) program, a "system of systems" approach to future air combat that includes a sixth-generation manned fighter jet accompanied by swarms of autonomous combat drones. The bill also accelerates the procurement of the new B-21 Raider long-range stealth bomber, seen as essential for projecting power across the vast distances of the Pacific.

The U.S. Navy is perhaps the single biggest beneficiary of the OBBB's largesse. The bill codifies the goal of growing the naval fleet to a minimum of 400 battle force ships, a dramatic increase from the fleet size of recent years. To achieve this, the legislation authorizes a multi-year block buy of Virginia-class fast-attack submarines and Arleigh Burke-class guided-missile destroyers, locking in production rates for years to come. It also fully funds the continued construction of the new Ford-class aircraft carriers and, crucially, provides the initial appropriations to begin replacing the aging Ohio-class ballistic missile submarines with the new, far more advanced Columbia-class, the most expensive shipbuilding program in the nation's history.

The U.S. Army sees its modernization efforts, which have been underway for several years, receive a powerful boost. The OBBB provides extensive funding to upgrade its armored brigades with new tanks and infantry fighting vehicles. It also makes a major investment in what the Army calls Long-Range Precision Fires, pouring money into the development and purchase of new missile and artillery systems capable of striking targets from hundreds of miles away. The Future Vertical Lift program, designed to replace the Army's aging helicopter fleet, including the venerable Black Hawk and Apache, also receives a significant increase in research and development funding to move its prototypes closer to production.

Even the newest branch of the military, the U.S. Space Force, sees its budget skyrocket under the OBBB. The bill allocates billions for the express purpose of achieving and maintaining "space superiority." This includes funding to launch a new constellation of highly resilient missile-warning and military communications satellites. It also directs significant resources toward developing capabilities to defend American satellites from attack and to counter the space-based systems of adversaries, a clear sign that the domain of space is now viewed as a potential future battlefield.

While buying new equipment grabs headlines, a substantial portion of the new defense funding is directed at a less glamorous but equally critical problem: readiness. For years, military leaders have warned Congress about readiness shortfalls, a term that encompasses a wide range of issues. It can mean Air Force jets that are not airworthy because of a lack of spare parts, Navy ships stuck in port awaiting overdue maintenance, or Army units not having enough training time to remain at peak proficiency. These shortfalls are the result of years of sustained combat operations combined with inconsistent budgets.

The OBBB tackles this problem head-on by pouring tens of billions of dollars into the military's Operations and Maintenance (O&M) accounts. This money is earmarked to clear the backlog at naval shipyards and aviation depots, allowing ships and aircraft to get the repairs they need to return to service. It funds the purchase of vast quantities of spare parts, from jet engines to tank treads, to replenish depleted stockpiles. The bill also increases funding for more realistic, large-scale training exercises and allows for more flying hours for pilots, ensuring that the force is not just well-equipped but also well-prepared to use that equipment effectively.

Beyond the hardware of today and the readiness of the force, the One Big Beautiful Bill makes a historic investment in the military of tomorrow. The funding allocated for Research, Development, Test, and Evaluation (RDT&E) is the largest in American history, even when adjusted for inflation. This part of the bill is designed to ensure that the United States maintains its technological edge over its competitors for decades to come. The goal is not just to improve existing systems but to spark breakthroughs that could fundamentally change the character of warfare.

Several key areas are targeted for this massive R&D investment. At the top of the list are hypersonic weapons. The bill allocates billions to accelerate both the development of offensive hypersonic missiles, which can travel at more than five times the speed of sound, and the creation of defensive systems capable of tracking and intercepting them. This reflects a sense of urgency in Washington to catch up with and surpass the progress made by China and Russia in this critical field.

Artificial intelligence (AI) is another major focus. The OBBB establishes several new research initiatives aimed at integrating AI and machine learning into every facet of military operations. This includes developing AI-powered tools for analyzing intelligence data, systems for coordinating the actions of autonomous drones and vehicles, and advanced algorithms to help commanders make faster and better decisions in the heat of battle. The bill's authors see mastery of military AI as essential to future victory.

The legislation also doubles down on investments in cyber warfare and directed energy. It provides a massive funding increase for U.S. Cyber Command to develop both more resilient defenses for military networks and more potent offensive cyber tools. At the same time, it boosts funding for once-futuristic directed-energy programs, such as high-powered lasers and microwave weapons, intended to shoot down drones, missiles, and even incoming artillery shells at a fraction of the cost of traditional interceptors.

The most expensive and long-term commitment in the entire defense package is the full funding of the comprehensive modernization of the nation's nuclear deterrent. The OBBB provides the necessary appropriations to keep all three legs of the nuclear triad on track for a complete overhaul. This includes continuing the development of the Sentinel intercontinental ballistic missile (ICBM) to replace the Minuteman III missiles that have stood watch in silos across the American heartland for half a century. It also includes the previously mentioned B-21 bomber and the Columbia-class submarine, both of which are primarily designed for their role in nuclear deterrence.

Finally, while the bulk of the new money is aimed at hardware and technology, the bill does address military personnel directly. It authorizes a 6.5 percent pay raise for all uniformed service members, the largest single-year increase in more than two decades. It also provides a significant boost in funding for the construction and renovation of military barracks and family housing, and increases the budgets for military healthcare and childcare services. These quality-of-life initiatives, which will be examined in much greater detail in a later chapter, were included to ensure that as the military invests in its machines, it does not neglect the men and women who operate them.

The sheer scale of this military buildup was, unsurprisingly, the subject of intense and deeply divided debate. Proponents of the OBBB argued that this level of investment was the bare minimum required to secure the nation in an increasingly hostile world. They contended that a strong and visible commitment to military power is the most effective way to deter potential adversaries from aggression, thereby preventing future conflicts before they can begin. They also pointed to the domestic economic benefits, arguing that the spending would support millions of high-paying jobs in the defense industry and its vast supply chain, while the

R&D funding would spur technological innovations that would eventually benefit the civilian economy.

Critics of the bill, on the other hand, described the spending increase as dangerously excessive and fiscally catastrophic. They argued that adding over a trillion dollars to the national debt to fund the Pentagon would ultimately make the country weaker, not stronger, by crowding out investments in other critical areas like education, infrastructure, and public health. They questioned whether the United States could or should continue to police the globe, arguing for a more restrained foreign policy that relied more on diplomacy and economic partnerships than on military force.

Furthermore, opponents warned that such a massive military buildup would inevitably trigger a new global arms race, compelling competitor nations to increase their own military spending in response, leading to a more volatile and dangerous world for everyone. Many raised the specter of the "military-industrial complex," a term famously used by President Dwight D. Eisenhower to describe the powerful alliance of defense contractors and politicians, suggesting that the massive spending increase was driven as much by lobbying and corporate profits as by any legitimate strategic need.

CHAPTER ELEVEN: Securing the Border: A Surge in Funding and Enforcement

Following its massive reinvestment in the Department of Defense, the One Big Beautiful Bill pivots to what its authors described as the nation's most pressing domestic security challenge: the southern border. The legislation treats the border not merely as a line on a map to be managed, but as a sovereign frontier to be sealed. It allocates a torrent of funding and a host of new authorities to the Department of Homeland Security (DHS), with the explicit goal of gaining "full operational control" over the nearly two-thousand-mile stretch dividing the United States from Mexico. This chapter details the three main pillars of this strategy: building the wall, deploying a new generation of technology, and hiring a small army of new enforcement agents.

The centerpiece of the OBBB's border security plan is the full and final funding for a contiguous border wall system. The bill appropriates an initial sum of seventy-five billion dollars dedicated exclusively to the design, acquisition of land, and construction of physical barriers. This funding is firewalled, meaning it cannot be reprogrammed or reallocated by future administrations for other purposes without an act of Congress. The legislation moves beyond abstract goals and sets specific, legally mandated targets for construction, requiring the completion of at least seven hundred miles of new primary and secondary wall systems within the next five years.

The bill is highly prescriptive about the nature of the wall itself. It mandates that the primary structure in most new sectors be a thirty-foot-tall steel bollard fence. These bollards—hollow steel posts filled with concrete and reinforced with rebar—are to be set deep into concrete footings. The design includes features intended to make it more difficult to climb or cut through, such as anti-climb plates at the very top. In certain designated high-traffic urban areas, the bill requires the construction of a double-wall system: the primary bollard fence backed by a second, often

70

different, type of barrier several hundred feet away, creating a heavily monitored enforcement zone between the two.

To ensure this construction schedule is met, the OBBB grants the Secretary of Homeland Security sweeping powers to waive any and all federal, state, or local laws deemed an impediment to the wall's rapid construction. This includes the waiver of dozens of landmark environmental laws, such as the National Environmental Policy Act, the Endangered Species Act, and the Clean Water Act. The provision is designed to bypass the years of environmental impact studies and litigation that have slowed previous construction efforts. Proponents argued this was a necessary step to address a national security crisis, while opponents decried it as an unprecedented assault on environmental protections.

The bill also streamlines the process for the government to acquire private land needed for the wall's path. It expands the federal government's eminent domain authority along the border, shortening the legal timelines for property seizure and capping the amounts that can be contested in court. The legislation establishes a special fund to compensate landowners, but it also creates a fast-track judicial process for resolving disputes that is heavily weighted in the government's favor. This provision was designed to overcome one of the most significant and time-consuming obstacles to completing a contiguous border barrier.

Recognizing that a physical wall is only as good as the technology watching over it, the OBBB pairs its investment in steel and concrete with a multi-billion-dollar appropriation for a "virtual wall" of advanced surveillance technology. The goal is to create a multi-layered sensor network that leaves no stretch of the border unwatched. This involves a massive expansion of existing programs and the deployment of new systems designed to detect, identify, and track any movement across the border in real time.

A key component of this virtual wall is the deployment of thousands of new Integrated Fixed Towers. These are tall, semi-autonomous surveillance towers equipped with a suite of advanced sensors. Each tower typically includes high-resolution electro-optical cameras for daytime surveillance, thermal imaging cameras for detecting heat signatures at night, and powerful long-range radar systems capable of detecting people and vehicles from miles away. The bill funds the placement of these towers to create overlapping fields of view, ensuring continuous coverage along vast stretches of the border.

The feeds from these towers, along with other sensors, are routed to centralized command centers where advanced software powered by artificial intelligence analyzes the data. The bill specifically funds the development and deployment of AI programs that can automatically detect and classify potential intrusions, distinguishing between animals, vehicles, and people. When the system flags an event, it automatically alerts the nearest Border Patrol agent, sending the precise coordinates and live video of the subjects to a handheld device or a screen in their vehicle.

Where fixed towers are impractical, such as in extremely rugged mountainous terrain, the bill funds a massive increase in the use of autonomous aerial surveillance. This includes a significant expansion of the fleet of large, high-altitude Predator B drones operated by Customs and Border Protection (CBP). These drones can patrol a designated area for more than twenty hours at a time, providing a persistent "eye in the sky." The bill also funds the purchase of thousands of smaller, more mobile drones that can be launched by agents in the field to investigate a sensor alert or track a group of individuals on the move.

The technological blanket extends down to the ground itself. The OBBB provides funding to deploy tens of thousands of new Unattended Ground Sensors (UGS) in remote areas. These small, often camouflaged devices can be seismic, detecting the vibrations of footsteps or vehicles, or passive infrared, detecting body heat. When triggered, they transmit a silent alarm to Border Patrol, allowing agents to intercept groups using remote trails and smuggling routes far from the wall and main roads.

Even official ports of entry—the legal crossing points for people and commerce—are slated for a major technological upgrade. The bill allocates billions to accelerate the deployment of biometric entry-exit systems at all land, air, and sea ports. This involves replacing older systems with advanced facial recognition technology to screen all foreign nationals entering and, for the first time on a universal scale, exiting the country. The goal is to create a comprehensive system to track visa overstays, a major source of illegal immigration.

To handle the increased flow of commercial traffic and stop the smuggling of drugs and contraband, the bill also funds a massive expansion of Non-Intrusive Inspection (NII) technology. This includes the installation of powerful new X-ray and Gamma-ray scanning systems capable of imaging an entire tractor-trailer or shipping container in a single pass. The legislation sets a target of scanning at least ninety percent of all commercial vehicles and seventy-five percent of all passenger vehicles entering the country through southern border ports of entry within three years.

The third and final pillar of the OBBB's border security strategy is a dramatic surge in enforcement personnel. The bill acknowledges that walls and technology are useless without sufficient manpower to respond to the information they provide. To that end, it authorizes and funds the hiring of an additional 15,000 Border Patrol agents over the next five years, an increase of more than seventy-five percent over the force's existing size. This represents one of the largest single expansions of a federal law enforcement agency in American history.

To meet this ambitious hiring target, the legislation includes several provisions designed to attract and retain new agents. It authorizes significant pay raises across the board for all Border Patrol personnel and establishes a new system of "hardship duty" bonuses for agents assigned to the most remote and desolate stretches of the border. It also streamlines the notoriously lengthy and difficult hiring process, including modifying the requirements for polygraph examinations, which have historically had a very high failure rate and were seen as a major bottleneck in recruitment.

The funding extends beyond salaries to cover the full cost of training and equipping this new generation of agents. The bill provides for a major expansion of the Border Patrol Academy in Artesia, New-Mexico, to handle the larger class sizes. It also allocates funds for new vehicles, communications equipment, body armor, and service weapons for the expanded force. The goal is to create a larger, better-paid, and better-equipped force capable of projecting a constant presence along the entire border.

In addition to expanding the Border Patrol, which operates between the ports of entry, the bill also authorizes the hiring of 5,000 new CBP Officers to staff the official ports. This increase in personnel is intended to handle the workload from the new biometric systems and vehicle scanners, reducing wait times for legal trade and travel while simultaneously improving security. These new officers will receive specialized training in detecting fraudulent documents, identifying suspicious behavior, and operating the new high-tech inspection equipment.

Beyond just increasing numbers, the OBBB grants new authorities to agents in the field. One of the most significant changes is a legislative prohibition on what has been termed "catch and release." The bill mandates that any individual apprehended between ports of entry who is not an unaccompanied minor must be detained until their immigration case can be adjudicated or they can be immediately removed from the country. This policy is designed to end the practice of releasing apprehended migrants into the U.S. interior with a future court date, a practice proponents claimed encouraged more illegal crossings.

To facilitate this new detention mandate, the bill funds the construction of a series of new, large-scale "consequence delivery centers" located in close proximity to the border. These are not intended to be long-term detention facilities, but rather high-efficiency processing hubs. Their purpose is to house individuals for a short period—typically 72 to 96 hours—while their identity is confirmed, they are biometrically enrolled in government databases, and they undergo an initial screening to determine if they are eligible for immediate removal from the country.

The OBBB also makes significant changes to the initial asylum screening process that occurs at these facilities. Under previous policy, individuals who expressed a fear of returning to their home country were entitled to a "credible fear" interview with an asylum officer. The OBBB raises the legal standard for passing this initial interview, requiring the individual to demonstrate a much higher probability that they will ultimately qualify for asylum. The bill's text redefines "credible fear" to require a showing that it is "more likely than not" that the applicant is eligible for protection, a much tougher standard than the "significant possibility" standard it replaced.

This change is intended to screen out what the bill's authors termed "frivolous" or "unmeritorious" asylum claims at the earliest possible stage. Individuals who fail to meet this new, higher credible fear standard are then subject to immediate expedited removal, a legal process that allows CBP to deport certain individuals without a full hearing before an immigration judge. The bill expands the categories of people who can be placed into expedited removal, further empowering agents at the border to carry out immediate deportations.

The public and political debate surrounding these provisions was, predictably, intense and deeply polarized. Proponents of the OBBB's border security plan hailed it as a long-overdue and necessary response to a decades-long crisis. They argued that a nation that cannot control its own borders is not truly a sovereign nation. The combination of a physical wall, advanced technology, and increased manpower, they contended, would finally give the government the tools it needed to stop the flow of illegal drugs like fentanyl, which has had a devastating impact on American communities.

Supporters also framed the bill as a matter of national security, arguing that a porous border represents a significant vulnerability that could be exploited by terrorists or foreign adversaries. They presented the high cost of the plan as a necessary investment in the safety and security of the American people, one that would pay for itself in the long run by reducing the fiscal and social costs associated with illegal immigration. The new, stricter enforcement policies were defended as essential measures to restore the rule of law and end the perceived abuse of the nation's asylum system.

On the other hand, a broad coalition of opponents sharply criticized the plan on humanitarian, fiscal, and environmental grounds. They described the wall as an expensive, ineffective, and environmentally destructive vanity project that would do little to stop determined migrants or sophisticated smuggling organizations, who would simply go over, under, or around it. The immense cost of the project was frequently highlighted, with critics arguing that the hundreds of billions of dollars being allocated to the border could be far more effectively spent on addressing the root causes of migration, such as poverty and violence in Central America.

Human rights organizations raised dire warnings about the impact of the new enforcement policies. They argued that raising the standard for credible fear interviews would result in the United States turning away legitimate refugees and sending them back to face persecution, torture, or death in their home countries, a violation of both U.S. and international law. The mandatory detention policy and the construction of massive new processing centers were condemned as measures that would lead to the widespread incarceration of vulnerable people, including families seeking safety.

Civil liberties groups voiced strong objections to the widespread expansion of surveillance technology. They warned that creating a system of constant, AI-monitored surveillance along the border could be a precursor to similar technologies being deployed within the country, threatening the privacy of all Americans. The waiver of environmental laws was met with lawsuits and protests from environmental groups, who argued that building a wall through fragile ecosystems and wildlife corridors would cause irreversible damage to the natural heritage of the borderlands. The debate encapsulated a fundamental disagreement about the character of the nation: whether its priority should be to build a fortress or to remain a beacon of hope.

CHAPTER TWELVE: A Nationwide Deportation Initiative: How It Works

While the towering steel bollards and advanced sensor networks detailed in the previous chapter are designed to fortify the nation's physical border, the One Big Beautiful Bill extends its immigration enforcement mandate far beyond the Rio Grande. The legislation launches one of the most ambitious and far-reaching interior immigration enforcement campaigns in American history. It moves the operational focus from the remote deserts and riverbanks of the frontier to the neighborhoods, workplaces, and communities in every state. This chapter will unpack the complex machinery of this nationwide deportation initiative, explaining how it is designed to work, who it targets, and the new powers it grants to the federal agents tasked with carrying it out.

At its core, the initiative is a directive to U.S. Immigration and Customs Enforcement (ICE), and specifically its Enforcement and Removal Operations (ERO) division, to dramatically increase the number of apprehensions and removals of undocumented immigrants living within the United States. The OBBB rejects the prosecutorial discretion models of previous administrations, which often prioritized the removal of recent arrivals and serious criminals. Instead, it statutorily broadens the categories of individuals deemed priorities for enforcement, effectively making nearly any person residing in the country without legal authorization a target for arrest and deportation.

The bill establishes a clear, tiered priority system. The highest priority remains individuals with serious criminal convictions, particularly aggravated felonies, and those deemed threats to national security. However, the legislation significantly expands this top tier to include anyone with a conviction for driving under the influence (DUI), regardless of how long ago it occurred, as well as anyone charged with, but not yet convicted of, any felony or serious misdemeanor. This shift from focusing on convictions to including charges is a significant expansion of the enforcement net.

The next priority tier includes any individual who has a final order of removal issued by an immigration judge but has not yet departed the country. This group is estimated to comprise hundreds of thousands of people, many of whom have lived in the U.S. for years, often checking in regularly with ICE as required. The OBBB directs ICE to clear this entire backlog of outstanding removal orders. The third and broadest tier includes anyone who has overstayed a valid visa or who entered the country without inspection, regardless of how long they have lived in the United States, whether they have American-born children, or if they have any criminal history.

To execute this sweeping mandate, the One Big Beautiful Bill provides ICE with a funding and staffing surge that mirrors the one given to the Border Patrol. The legislation appropriates an additional forty billion dollars to ICE over the next five years, specifically for interior enforcement. It also authorizes the hiring of 12,000 new ERO officers, a move that would more than double the size of the agency's existing deportation force. This massive increase in personnel is intended to allow ICE to stand up new field offices across the country and dramatically increase the pace and scale of its enforcement operations.

A significant portion of the new funding is earmarked for a massive expansion of the nation's immigration detention capacity. The bill directs the agency to increase the number of available detention beds from its historical average of around 40,000 to a new baseline of 100,000. To achieve this, the OBBB provides funds for the construction of several new, large-scale federal detention centers. It also streamlines the process for ICE to enter into contracts with private prison corporations and county jails, encouraging a rapid build-out of detention space through public-private partnerships. This expansion is essential to fulfilling the bill's mandate to detain nearly all apprehended individuals until their removal.

The process of finding and arresting millions of people scattered across a vast nation requires a sophisticated identification system. The OBBB creates this system by mandating unprecedented levels of data sharing between government agencies. The legislation makes participation in the Secure Communities program mandatory for all state and local law enforcement agencies nationwide. This program automatically runs the fingerprints of every person arrested for any crime—from a traffic violation to a serious felony—against federal immigration databases. If a match occurs, ICE is automatically notified, and the local jail is instructed to hold the individual until ICE agents can take them into custody.

The bill goes further by requiring the Social Security Administration, the Internal Revenue Service, and the Department of Labor to provide ICE with direct access to their databases. The stated purpose is to allow ICE to identify non-citizens who are working without authorization by cross-referencing employment records with immigration status. The legislation also funds the development of new data-mining software that uses artificial intelligence to sift through vast amounts of public and government records to identify individuals who are likely in the country illegally, creating lists of potential targets for ERO officers.

Once an individual is identified, the next step is apprehension. The OBBB gives ERO officers enhanced authority to make arrests. It creates a new form of administrative warrant, issued not by a judge but by an ICE supervisor, which authorizes agents to enter a person's home or workplace to make an arrest. While the constitutionality of such warrants has long been debated, the bill attempts to codify this power into law. The new funding also supports a dramatic increase in large-scale worksite enforcement operations, where ICE agents raid businesses suspected of hiring undocumented workers, as well as "at-large" arrests in community settings.

After an individual is taken into custody, the OBBB's new procedures are designed for speed and efficiency, with the primary goal being rapid removal. The bill significantly expands the use of a process called "expedited removal." Previously, this fast-track deportation process, which bypasses an immigration judge, was primarily used for individuals apprehended at or near the border shortly after they entered. The new law expands expedited removal to apply to any undocumented individual anywhere in the country who cannot prove to an officer's satisfaction that they have been continuously present in the U.S. for at least two years.

This change means that a person arrested in the interior, for example, during a traffic stop in a state far from the border, could be questioned, processed, and deported in a matter of days or even hours, without ever seeing a judge. The burden of proof is placed entirely on the individual to immediately produce documents, like rental agreements or tax returns, to prove their long-term residency. If they cannot, they can be summarily removed. Proponents argued this is a necessary tool to quickly remove individuals with no legal claim to be in the country, while critics warned it creates a high risk of erroneous deportations of people who might have been eligible for some form of relief.

For those who are not subject to expedited removal, the bill still seeks to accelerate the adjudication process. It provides funding to hire hundreds of new immigration judges and create dozens of new immigration courts. However, these new courts are designed to operate more like high-volume processing centers. The bill imposes strict new deadlines on every stage of a case, limiting the time attorneys have to prepare, restricting the number of continuances a judge can grant, and curtailing the types of evidence that can be presented. The legislation also narrows the legal grounds for asylum and other forms of humanitarian relief, making it much more difficult for individuals to win their cases.

A cornerstone of the nationwide deportation initiative is its strategy for dealing with so-called "sanctuary jurisdictions." These are cities, counties, and states that have policies limiting their cooperation with federal immigration authorities. The OBBB takes a hardline approach to eliminating these policies. The bill makes any state or local jurisdiction that refuses to honor an ICE detainer—a request to hold an individual for up to 48 hours beyond their scheduled release so ICE can take custody—ineligible for a broad range of federal Justice Department and Homeland Security grants. This uses the power of the federal purse to compel cooperation.

The bill also resurrects and dramatically expands the 287(g) program. This program allows the Department of Homeland Security to enter into agreements with state and local police departments, delegating federal immigration enforcement authority to selected local officers. These deputized officers are trained by ICE and are empowered to question individuals about their immigration status, issue administrative warrants, and initiate deportation proceedings. The OBBB provides significant funding for this program, with the stated goal of creating 287(g) agreements in every state, effectively turning thousands of local police officers and sheriff's deputies into a force multiplier for ICE.

The final stage of the process is the physical removal of the individual from the United States. To handle the massive increase in deportations envisioned by the bill, the legislation provides a major funding boost for ICE Air Operations. This is the division of ICE that manages a fleet of chartered aircraft—essentially a government-run airline dedicated to deportations. The new funding allows for the chartering of more and larger aircraft and an increase in the number of removal flights to countries around the world. The bill also streamlines the process for obtaining travel documents from foreign countries that are often reluctant to accept the return of their nationals.

The debate surrounding this nationwide deportation initiative was one of the most visceral and emotional of the entire OBBB legislative process. Proponents argued that the plan represented a long-overdue commitment to enforcing the nation's laws as they are written. They framed the initiative as a matter of public safety, emphasizing that it would lead to the removal of thousands of individuals with criminal records. They also contended that restoring the rule of law to the immigration system was a matter of fairness to the millions of people who have waited patiently in line to immigrate to the country legally.

Supporters also made an economic case, arguing that removing a large population of unauthorized workers would open up jobs for American citizens and legal residents, potentially driving up wages in certain sectors of the economy. They presented the high cost of the initiative as a necessary investment that would be offset by future savings in social services, education, and healthcare. The crackdown on sanctuary cities was defended as a critical measure to prevent dangerous individuals from being released back into communities.

Opponents, however, depicted the initiative as a fiscally irresponsible and morally bankrupt policy that would inflict immense human suffering. They argued that the plan would lead to the separation of hundreds of thousands of families, tearing parents from their American-citizen children and devastating communities. Immigrant rights groups and civil libertarians warned that the expanded powers granted to ICE and the pressure on local police to engage in immigration enforcement would inevitably lead to widespread racial profiling and a deep erosion of trust between law enforcement and the communities they are sworn to protect.

Economists and business groups, particularly in the agriculture, construction, and hospitality industries, voiced strong opposition, warning that the mass removal of a significant portion of their workforce would have a catastrophic impact on their businesses and the broader economy. They argued that there were not enough native-born workers willing to take these often difficult and low-paying jobs, and that a mass deportation campaign would lead to labor shortages, rising prices for consumers, and a potential economic recession.

Human rights organizations condemned the expansion of expedited removal and the new restrictions on asylum, arguing that these provisions would put vulnerable people at risk and violate the United States' long-standing commitments under international law to protect refugees. The sheer logistics and cost of apprehending, detaining, and transporting millions of people were also called into question, with critics suggesting that the plan was not only cruel but also practically unworkable, a recipe for chaos, and a gross misuse of taxpayer dollars that could be better spent on other national priorities.

CHAPTER THIRTEEN: The End of Green Energy Tax Credits as We Know Them

For more than a decade, the federal government's approach to energy policy resembled that of a gardener tending a prized new plant. It provided a complex trellis of tax credits, subsidies, and incentives designed to nurture the growth of the green energy sector. From the solar panels on a suburban rooftop to the towering wind turbines on a Texas plain, and even to the electric car in the driveway, a federal tax credit was often part of the financial equation, encouraging investment and adoption. The One Big Beautiful Bill does not just prune this trellis; it pulls it up from the roots, fundamentally altering the financial landscape for renewable energy in America.

This chapter of the bill represents a complete philosophical reversal from the policies of the preceding years, most notably those enacted in the Inflation Reduction Act (IRA) of 2022. That legislation had created or expanded a vast array of credits with the dual goals of combating climate change and building a domestic clean energy manufacturing base. The OBBB operates on the premise that these incentives have distorted the free market, unfairly picked winners and losers, and placed an unnecessary burden on the American taxpayer. It seeks to end this era of government support, arguing that these technologies should now sink or swim on their own economic merits.

The bill accomplishes this not through one single action, but through a multi-pronged assault on the existing tax code. For some credits, it enacts an immediate and total repeal. For others, it drastically accelerates their scheduled phase-out, effectively pulling the plug years ahead of schedule. And for the largest industrial credits, it claws back their value and eliminates the long-term certainty that is the lifeblood of major energy projects. The cumulative effect is the dismantling of the most significant federal support structure for clean energy in the nation's history.

Perhaps the most visible and immediate impact for the average consumer is the sudden elimination of the tax credit for new and used electric vehicles, often referred to as EVs. Under the previous law, a buyer could receive a tax credit of up to $7,500 for the purchase of a qualifying new electric vehicle, with a smaller credit of up to $4,000 available for used EVs. These credits, which had complex sourcing and manufacturing requirements, were designed to make EVs more price-competitive with their gasoline-powered counterparts and to spur a domestic EV supply chain.

The OBBB repeals these credits, effective immediately upon the president's signature. There is no phase-out period and no grandfather clause for customers who may have placed an order but not yet taken delivery. From one day to the next, the final cost of purchasing a new EV for millions of Americans will increase by the full amount of the former credit. This represents one of the most direct and abrupt policy-driven price hikes for a consumer good in recent memory.

The rationale offered by the bill's sponsors was straightforward. They argued that the EV tax credit disproportionately benefited wealthier households who were more likely to purchase new cars. It was, in their view, a federal subsidy for a lifestyle choice, and one that unfairly disadvantaged buyers of traditional gasoline vehicles. Furthermore, they contended that the EV market was now mature enough to compete without government assistance, pointing to the growing number of models available and the increasing consumer interest. The policy was framed as an end to "corporate welfare" for auto manufacturers and a victory for market freedom.

Opponents of this change painted a very different picture. They argued that the EV market is still in its nascent stages, with electric vehicles representing only a fraction of total cars on the road. The credit, they claimed, was essential for helping the industry achieve the scale necessary to bring down costs for everyone. They warned that its repeal would stifle EV adoption, slow the transition away from foreign oil, and severely damage the competitiveness of American automakers who have invested billions of dollars in new

EV factories based on the assumption that these credits would remain in place. They also pointed out that the domestic content requirements in the old credits were specifically designed to onshore manufacturing jobs, a goal the repeal now undermines.

The OBBB extends this same logic from the driveway to the rooftop. The bill targets the suite of residential clean energy credits that encouraged homeowners to invest in solar panels, battery storage systems, geothermal heat pumps, and other energy-efficient home upgrades. The most prominent of these was the Residential Clean Energy Credit, which allowed a homeowner to subtract 30% of the total cost of installing a new solar energy system directly from their federal tax bill. For a typical $25,000 rooftop solar installation, this amounted to a $7,500 tax credit.

Instead of an immediate repeal, the bill enacts a rapid and severe phase-down of this and related residential credits. Under the new law, the credit percentage is slashed from 30% to 15% for the next tax year. The year after that, it is cut again to just 7.5%. In the third year, it disappears completely. This legislative cliff is designed to wean homeowners and the residential solar industry off the subsidy in short order.

The argument for this change was that residential solar has become significantly cheaper over the past decade and should no longer require a hefty taxpayer-funded incentive. Proponents claimed the credit was another example of a subsidy that primarily benefited higher-income homeowners who could afford the upfront cost of such an installation. By phasing it out, they argued, the government would be treating all forms of home energy more equitably and saving billions in tax revenue.

The residential solar industry and environmental advocates strongly opposed this move. They argued that while solar costs have come down, the 30% credit was often the deciding factor that made the investment financially viable for middle-class families. They predicted that the rapid phase-out would cause a dramatic contraction in the residential solar market, leading to significant job losses among the nation's thousands of solar installation companies, most of which are small, local businesses. They also contended that distributed rooftop solar is a key component of building a more resilient and less centralized electrical grid, a goal the new policy actively discourages.

While the consumer-facing credits were the most visible targets, the most financially significant rollbacks in the OBBB are aimed at the massive tax incentives that underpin the utility-scale renewable energy industry. For decades, the growth of America's wind and solar farms has been driven by two key policy tools: the Production Tax Credit (PTC) and the Investment Tax Credit (ITC). The PTC provides a per-kilowatt-hour credit for electricity generated by a renewable facility for its first ten years of operation, rewarding production. The ITC provides an upfront credit based on a percentage of the project's total investment cost, rewarding capital deployment.

The Inflation Reduction Act had supercharged these credits, extending them for a decade and increasing their value, particularly for projects that used American-made components or were built in traditional energy communities. This provided the long-term certainty that developers and financiers need to undertake massive, multi-billion-dollar energy projects that can take years to plan and build. The OBBB systematically dismantles this entire framework.

The bill immediately repeals all the "bonus" credit amounts from the IRA. The domestic content adders and other incentives are eliminated overnight. More critically, the legislation reverts the base credit amounts for the ITC and PTC to their lower, pre-IRA levels and, most importantly, imposes a hard, final expiration date at the end of the next calendar year. Any project that has not "commenced construction" by that deadline will be completely ineligible for either credit.

This legislative maneuver effectively slams the window shut on new large-scale renewable energy development. The long lead times involved in siting, permitting, and financing wind and solar farms mean that this new, near-term deadline makes it practically impossible to get new projects off the ground. It replaces a decade of policy certainty with a one-year countdown to termination.

The sponsors of the OBBB defended this as a necessary correction. They argued that the PTC and ITC have been in place for more than thirty years and have long outlived their original purpose of jump-starting a new industry. In their view, wind and solar are now mature, cost-competitive sources of electricity in many parts of the country and should compete with fossil fuels on a level playing field, free from what they termed "perpetual subsidies." The move was presented as a major step toward restoring market neutrality in the energy sector and ending a massive category of corporate tax expenditures.

The renewable energy industry and its supporters reacted with alarm, describing the move as a catastrophic blow that would create chaos in energy markets. They argued that the long-term credits were essential for leveling the playing field against fossil fuels, which they claim have their own long history of government support. They warned that the sudden termination of the credits would cause a collapse in new renewable project development, jeopardizing the nation's ability to meet future electricity demand and increasing its reliance on volatile natural gas markets. Major investors, from pension funds to multinational banks, warned that the policy uncertainty created by the bill would drive capital away from the U.S. energy sector and toward countries with more stable renewable energy policies.

The final piece of the OBBB's green energy rollback strategy is aimed squarely at the future of the clean energy supply chain. The IRA had included a suite of powerful manufacturing tax credits—known as 45X credits—specifically designed to incentivize companies to build factories in the United States to produce solar panels, wind turbine components, EV batteries, and process critical minerals. The goal was to break the nation's reliance on Chinese manufacturing for these key technologies and to create thousands of American factory jobs. Dozens of new facilities were announced across the country in the wake of these credits being enacted.

The One Big Beautiful Bill repeals the 45X manufacturing credits entirely. The repeal is not phased in; it is immediate and absolute. For companies that had already begun construction on new factories in reliance on these credits, the financial basis for their investment vanishes overnight.

The stated reason for this repeal was ideological consistency. Proponents of the OBBB argued that the government should not be in the business of industrial planning. They contended that these credits were a form of protectionism that would lead to inefficiency and that the market, not Washington, should decide where it is most economical to build factories and source components. The focus, they claimed, should be on broad-based tax relief that helps all manufacturers, not targeted subsidies for politically favored green industries.

Critics of the repeal described it as a unilateral economic disarmament. They argued that it was a grave strategic error to cede the manufacturing of the world's next generation of energy technology to competitor nations, particularly China, which heavily subsidizes its own industries. They warned that the repeal would lead to the immediate cancellation of many planned factory projects, vaporizing tens of thousands of potential manufacturing jobs in communities across the country, many of them in the so-called "battery belt" in the American South and Midwest. For them, this was not just an energy policy decision, but a national security and economic competitiveness blunder of the first order.

The bill also eliminates a host of smaller, more specialized green energy incentives. Tax credits for commercial EV charging stations, sustainable aviation fuel, and clean hydrogen production are all either repealed or set on a path to rapid expiration. The overarching message sent by the legislation is clear and unambiguous: the era of federal financial support for the transition to a low-carbon economy is over. From this point forward, wind, solar, and electric vehicles are on their own, left to compete in a marketplace where, as the next chapter will detail, the federal government is now placing its thumb firmly on the other side of the scale.

CHAPTER FOURTEEN: Unleashing American Energy: A New Focus on Oil, Gas, and Coal

If the previous chapter detailed the One Big Beautiful Bill's demolition of the federal support structure for green energy, this chapter explains what the bill builds in its place. The legislation does not simply create a neutral, free-market playing field. Instead, it enacts a suite of policies designed to aggressively promote the exploration, production, and consumption of American fossil fuels. The guiding principle is a concept the bill's authors termed "energy dominance." This is not merely energy independence, but a strategy to maximize the extraction of the nation's oil, natural gas, and coal resources for both domestic use and global export. The OBBB achieves this through three primary mechanisms: unlocking federal lands, dismantling regulations, and providing powerful new financial incentives.

The first and most direct action is a fundamental rewrite of the rules governing energy production on land and in waters owned by the federal government. For decades, the process of leasing these areas for oil and gas drilling has been a contentious tug-of-war involving federal agencies, energy companies, and environmental groups, often resulting in lengthy delays and litigation. The OBBB aims to cut through this Gordian knot by replacing bureaucratic discretion with legislative command. The bill mandates that the Department of the Interior conduct a minimum of four offshore oil and gas lease sales and four onshore lease sales in multiple states every single year.

This mandate effectively ends the ability of any presidential administration to pause or slow down the pace of federal leasing. It transforms the process from a discretionary activity into a statutory obligation. If the Interior Department fails to offer a sufficient number of acres for lease in a given quarter, the bill prohibits it from issuing any permits for renewable energy projects, such as offshore wind farms, on federal lands or waters. This provision creates a powerful incentive for the bureaucracy to prioritize fossil fuel development, effectively holding renewable projects hostage to ensure the oil and gas leasing schedule is met.

To accelerate the path from leasing to drilling, the OBBB launches a full-scale assault on the permitting process. The cornerstone of this effort is a dramatic overhaul of the National Environmental Policy Act (NEPA), a half-century-old law that requires federal agencies to study the environmental consequences of their major actions. The bill imposes a hard, two-year time limit on the completion of any environmental impact statement for an energy project. For less complex projects requiring only an environmental assessment, the deadline is set at one year. These are not targets; they are legally binding deadlines.

The legislation also significantly narrows the scope of what these reviews must consider. It directs agencies to focus only on environmental effects that are "reasonably foreseeable" and have a "close causal relationship" to the proposed project. This language is specifically designed to exclude the consideration of broader, cumulative impacts, most notably a project's contribution to global climate change. Furthermore, the bill sharply curtails the ability of citizens and environmental groups to challenge energy projects in court. It shortens the statute of limitations for filing lawsuits and raises the legal standing required to bring a case, making it much more difficult for opponents to block or delay a project through litigation.

The sponsors of these reforms championed them as a war on red tape. They argued that the old permitting system had become a weaponized tool for obstruction, miring essential energy projects in years of paperwork and frivolous lawsuits. By streamlining reviews and limiting litigation, they contended, the bill would unleash billions of dollars in private investment, create thousands of high-paying jobs, and lower energy prices for American consumers. The promise was a faster, more predictable process that would restore certainty for energy producers and make the United States a more attractive place to invest.

Critics, however, described these changes as a bulldozer driving through the nation's bedrock environmental laws. They argued that the arbitrary time limits would force agencies to rubber-stamp projects without a thorough and scientifically rigorous analysis of their potential harms. Rushing these complex reviews, they claimed, would lead to more oil spills, more air and water pollution, and more damage to sensitive ecosystems and wildlife. They viewed the restrictions on legal challenges not as a move to stop frivolous lawsuits, but as an attempt to silence the voices of local communities, ranchers, and indigenous groups whose land and livelihoods could be directly impacted by these projects.

The second major pillar of the OBBB's energy strategy is the systematic dismantling of existing environmental regulations that the bill's authors deemed overly burdensome to the fossil fuel industry. Where the first pillar cleared the way for future production, this one provides immediate relief to current operations. The most significant of these rollbacks is the complete repeal of the Methane Emissions Reduction Program, which had been established just a few years prior. This program was designed to levy a fee on excessive methane leaks from oil and gas wells, pipelines, and storage facilities.

Methane is the primary component of natural gas, but it is also a greenhouse gas over eighty times more potent than carbon dioxide in the short term. The fee was intended to create a strong financial incentive for energy companies to invest in modern equipment and practices to plug leaks and reduce venting and flaring. The OBBB eliminates this fee entirely before it could fully take effect. The bill's proponents argued that the fee was a punitive tax that would have driven up energy costs and that the industry was already making voluntary progress on reducing methane emissions through technological innovation.

Opponents of the repeal called it a reckless and irresponsible giveaway to polluters. They pointed to scientific studies showing that methane emissions from the oil and gas sector were far higher than previously estimated and represented a major driver of climate change. The fee, they argued, was the most cost-effective tool available for achieving rapid and significant reductions in these emissions. Its repeal, they warned, would lock in higher levels of pollution for years to come and represent a major setback in efforts to address global warming.

The regulatory rollback extends from the oilfield to the power plant. The bill repeals or weakens several key Clean Air Act regulations that govern emissions from coal- and natural gas-fired power plants. It specifically targets rules related to mercury, coal ash, and cross-state air pollution. The legislation also provides power plant operators with greater flexibility, allowing them to make significant upgrades to their facilities without triggering the "New Source Review" process, a provision that normally requires plants to install modern pollution controls when they make major modifications.

This package of regulatory changes was defended as a common-sense move to lower electricity costs and improve grid reliability. Supporters argued that the existing regulations were forcing the premature retirement of perfectly good power plants, particularly coal-fired ones, threatening the stability of the nation's electricity supply. By providing this relief, they contended, the bill would keep affordable power plants online, ensuring that Americans have access to reliable and low-cost electricity.

Environmental and public health advocates strongly condemned these provisions. They argued that weakening these rules would directly result in more air pollution and, consequently, higher rates of asthma, heart disease, and other respiratory illnesses, particularly in communities located near power plants. They presented evidence that the targeted regulations had already produced billions of dollars in public health benefits that far outweighed their compliance costs. The rollback, they claimed, was a transfer of wealth from the public—in the form of increased health costs—to the shareholders of utility companies.

The third and final pillar of the OBBB's fossil fuel strategy is a suite of new and enhanced tax incentives. While the bill was busy eliminating credits for green energy, it was also creating new ones for oil, gas, and coal. It codifies and makes permanent a host of long-standing tax deductions that have been mainstays of the oil and gas industry for decades. These include the ability to immediately deduct "intangible drilling costs," such as labor, fuel, and repairs associated with drilling a new well, and the "percentage depletion" allowance, which allows independent producers to deduct a flat percentage of the revenue from a well, regardless of their actual investment costs.

Proponents have long defended these provisions as essential for encouraging high-risk domestic energy exploration. They argue that drilling for oil is an expensive and speculative venture and that these tax rules are necessary to attract the capital needed to find and develop new reserves. Making them a permanent and unshakable part of the tax code, they claimed, provides the industry with the stability it needs to make long-term investments.

Critics, however, have long derided these provisions as antiquated and unnecessary subsidies for a mature and highly profitable industry. They argue that these tax breaks give the fossil fuel industry a permanent competitive advantage over other sectors of the economy. The non-partisan Congressional Budget Office and other watchdog groups have for years included the repeal of these deductions on their lists of options for reducing the federal deficit.

Beyond solidifying old tax breaks, the OBBB creates a major new one aimed squarely at making coal and natural gas power plants more appealing in a carbon-conscious world. The legislation dramatically expands and enhances the tax credit for carbon capture, utilization, and storage (CCUS) technology. These systems are designed to capture carbon dioxide emissions at the source—such as the smokestack of a power plant—and either transport it via pipeline for use in other industrial processes or inject it deep underground for permanent storage.

Under the new law, the value of the tax credit, known as 45Q, is significantly increased for every ton of carbon that is captured and stored. The bill also makes the credit "directly refundable," meaning a company can receive it as a cash payment from the government, even if it has no tax liability. This makes the subsidy much more valuable and easier to monetize. The goal of this enhanced credit is to spur a massive private investment in building out CCUS infrastructure, thereby creating a potential lifeline for fossil fuel power plants that would otherwise be facing pressure to shut down due to their carbon emissions.

The bill's sponsors presented this as a pragmatic, innovation-focused approach to climate change. They argued that instead of punishing fossil fuels, the government should invest in technologies that can make them cleaner. Carbon capture, they contended, allows the nation to continue benefiting from its abundant and affordable coal and gas resources while still reducing greenhouse gas emissions. They positioned it as an "all-of-the-above" energy solution that bridges the gap between economic reality and environmental goals.

Many environmental groups, however, viewed the enhanced credit with deep skepticism. They have long argued that CCUS technology is exorbitantly expensive, has a poor track record of success at scale, and serves primarily as a pretext to prolong the life of polluting power plants. They warned that the massive new subsidy would divert billions of dollars toward propping up the fossil fuel industry that could be more effectively spent on deploying proven, zero-emission technologies like wind and solar. They labeled the policy a "boondoggle" that would fail to deliver its promised climate benefits while locking in fossil fuel infrastructure for decades to come.

Finally, the One Big Beautiful Bill takes specific action to shore up the nation's ailing coal industry. The legislation repeals a moratorium on new federal coal leasing that had been in place for years, opening up vast new tracts of publicly owned land, particularly in the Powder River Basin of Wyoming and Montana, for future coal mining. The bill also provides funding for research and development into "advanced coal" technologies, with the goal of creating more efficient coal-fired power plants.

These measures were championed as a long-overdue lifeline for coal country, the communities in Appalachia and the West that have been devastated by the decline of the coal industry. Proponents argued that coal remains a vital component of a reliable energy grid and that the federal government has a responsibility to support the miners and communities that have powered the nation for generations. They framed the bill as a fulfillment of a promise to "bring back coal."

To opponents, these provisions represented a futile and environmentally damaging attempt to reverse an unstoppable economic and technological trend. They argued that coal is no longer competitive with cheaper natural gas and renewables, and that no amount of government support can change that fundamental market reality. They contended that propping up a declining industry was a waste of taxpayer money and that the focus should instead be on investing in economic diversification and providing a just transition for the workers and communities impacted by the shift away from coal.

CHAPTER FIFTEEN: Reshaping Agriculture: New Subsidies and Support for Farmers

American agriculture operates on a scale that is often difficult to comprehend. It is a world of immense productivity and immense risk, where a farmer's entire year of work can be wiped out by a single hailstorm, a summer-long drought, or a sudden collapse in global commodity prices. For nearly a century, the federal government has played the role of an essential, if often complicated, business partner to the American farmer, providing a safety net of subsidies, insurance, and conservation programs. The One Big Beautiful Bill does not fire this business partner, but it does rewrite the partnership agreement in its entirety, shifting the focus away from the complex, conservation-linked programs of the recent past and towards a simpler, more direct, and aggressively production-oriented model of support.

While other parts of the OBBB, such as the estate tax reforms detailed in an earlier chapter, provide significant long-term benefits for the transfer of family farms to the next generation, this chapter of the bill deals with the nuts and bolts of farming itself. It overhauls the core farm bill programs that affect the annual balance sheet of nearly every agricultural producer in the country, from the corn fields of Iowa to the dairy barns of Wisconsin and the cotton fields of the Mississippi Delta. The new philosophy is unambiguous: the primary job of the American farmer is to produce, and the primary job of the federal government is to make it as profitable and predictable as possible for them to do so.

The centerpiece of this new approach is a program the bill christens the "American Harvest Security Program." This new initiative sweeps away the alphabet soup of programs that came before it, most notably the Price Loss Coverage (PLC) and Agriculture Risk Coverage (ARC) programs, which had formed the core of the farm safety net for the previous decade. The stated goal of the American Harvest Security Program is to offer farmers simplicity and bankable certainty in a world of volatile markets. It achieves this by establishing a new, politically determined support price for a handful of key commodity crops: corn, soybeans, wheat, cotton, and rice.

This support price, which the bill calls the "National Strategic Reserve Price," is the lynchpin of the entire program. It is set at a level significantly higher than the average market prices seen over the last several years. The bill effectively creates a high, solid price floor for the nation's most widely grown crops. If the national average market price for, say, corn falls below this new strategic price at the end of the marketing year, any farmer who has historically planted corn receives a direct payment from the federal government to make up the difference. The payment is calculated based on their farm's established yield history and acreage, providing a guaranteed baseline revenue stream.

This model is a deliberate departure from the more complex revenue-based programs it replaces. By tying payments to a fixed national price rather than a farm's individual revenue, the OBBB aims to reduce paperwork and make the safety net easier to understand. The bill's proponents argued that this provides farmers with a clear, unambiguous price signal that they and their bankers can rely on when making planting and investment decisions for the coming year. It was presented as a program designed not to micromanage risk, but to eliminate the worst-case scenario of a catastrophic price collapse for the foundational crops of American agriculture.

The second major pillar of the new farm safety net is a significant enhancement of the Federal Crop Insurance Program. This public-private partnership, in which the federal government subsidizes the premiums farmers pay to private companies for crop insurance policies, has long been the most important risk management tool for most producers. The OBBB doubles down on this model, increasing the federal subsidy share for the most comprehensive types of insurance policies. The bill makes it significantly cheaper for a farmer to purchase a policy that covers 85% or even 90% of their expected crop revenue.

The argument behind this change is that it empowers farmers to take control of their own risk management. Instead of relying on direct government payments after a disaster strikes, farmers are incentivized to use a market-based tool to protect themselves beforehand. By making the highest levels of coverage more affordable, the bill encourages producers to insulate themselves from losses due to bad weather, pests, or other natural causes. It is a policy designed to reduce the need for Congress to pass expensive, ad-hoc disaster relief bills every time a hurricane or drought hits a major agricultural region.

However, to counter the argument that this was simply a giveaway to the private insurance companies that sell and service these policies, the OBBB includes a provision designed to ensure they have more "skin in the game." The legislation slightly increases the total amount of financial risk that the private insurance companies are required to retain on their books. This change modestly reduces their ability to pass all major, widespread losses directly back to the federal government's reinsurance fund. It was a concession to fiscal conservatives, framed as a pro-market reform that ensures the private sector partners share in the risk, not just the profits.

While the bill bolsters the financial safety net, it takes a radically different approach to conservation. The OBBB initiates a wholesale pivot in federal conservation policy, moving away from programs that prioritize environmental benefits as a primary goal and toward a model where conservation is valued mainly for its contribution to agricultural productivity. This is most evident in the bill's treatment of the major "working lands" conservation programs, such as the Environmental Quality Incentives Program (EQIP) and the Conservation Stewardship Program (CSP).

The OBBB consolidates these and several smaller programs into a new, streamlined entity called the "Productive Lands Enhancement Program," or PLEP. The name itself signals the change in philosophy. Under the old system, funding was often directed toward projects with clear environmental benefits, such as restoring wildlife habitat or implementing practices to sequester carbon in the soil to combat climate change. The new PLEP, by contrast, is statutorily directed to prioritize projects that have a direct, demonstrable, and positive impact on a farm's long-term productivity and profitability.

For example, under the new program, a farmer seeking federal cost-share assistance to upgrade their irrigation system from an old, inefficient model to a modern, water-saving one would be a top funding priority. The project saves water, which is an environmental benefit, but its primary justification in the eyes of PLEP is that it lowers the farmer's water and electricity costs and ensures a more reliable water supply to boost crop yields. Similarly, funding for precision agriculture technology that allows for the more targeted application of fertilizer would be prioritized because it reduces a farmer's input costs, with the corresponding reduction in nutrient runoff into streams and rivers seen as a secondary co-benefit.

This philosophical shift is even more stark in the bill's treatment of the Conservation Reserve Program (CRP). This program, one of the oldest and most popular conservation tools, pays farmers an annual rent to take their most environmentally sensitive land out of production and plant it with grasses or trees. The OBBB places a hard cap on the total national acreage that can be enrolled in the CRP, lowering it to a maximum of 20 million acres, a significant reduction from the levels of previous years. The bill's sponsors justified this by arguing that in a world facing growing food demand, productive American farmland should be used for growing crops, not left idle at taxpayer expense.

The OBBB also extends its new production-focused philosophy to the livestock and dairy sectors. For the nation's dairy farmers, who have long struggled with intense price volatility, the bill makes significant and politically important changes to the Dairy Margin Coverage (DMC) program. This is a safety-net program that makes payments to farmers when the national margin—the difference between the all-milk price and the average feed cost—falls below a certain level. The OBBB enhances this program by making the highest and most protective tiers of coverage more affordable for the nation's largest dairy operations, not just the smaller farms that previous versions of the program had tended to favor.

This change acknowledges the economic reality of the modern dairy industry, where a majority of the nation's milk is now produced by a shrinking number of very large, highly efficient farms. By providing a stronger safety net for these larger operations, the bill aims to bring more stability to the entire dairy supply chain. For ranchers, the OBBB streamlines and expands the key disaster assistance programs. It broadens the definitions of eligible loss events under the Livestock Indemnity Program, which compensates ranchers for animal deaths due to adverse weather or predators, and it creates a faster, less bureaucratic process for producers to file claims and receive payments after suffering losses from blizzards, floods, or wildfires.

In its quest to boost production, the One Big Beautiful Bill also seeks to accelerate the adoption of new agricultural technologies by dismantling regulatory barriers. The legislation creates a new "fast-track" approval pathway at the U.S. Department of Agriculture for new plant varieties developed using certain advanced gene-editing techniques, such as CRISPR. Under this new system, these crops would be presumed to be as safe as their conventionally bred cousins and would not be subject to the lengthy and expensive regulatory review process that applies to older forms of genetically modified organisms (GMOs). The burden of proof would be shifted to the agency, which would have to prove a potential risk within a strict 180-day review period to slow down a product's path to market.

Given that over ninety percent of the crops supported by the new American Harvest Security Program are sold overseas, the OBBB also includes several measures designed to bolster agricultural exports. The bill triples the annual funding for two long-standing export promotion programs, the Market Access Program (MAP) and the Foreign Market Development (FMD) program. These programs provide matching funds to agricultural trade associations to help them advertise and promote American-grown products in foreign markets, from U.S. beef in Japan to California almonds in India.

More aggressively, the OBBB creates a new "Agricultural Trade Retaliation Fund." This multi-billion-dollar fund gives the Secretary of Agriculture the authority to make direct payments to farmers who have been specifically targeted by retaliatory tariffs from other countries during a trade dispute. The goal is to create a financial shield for American agriculture, strengthening the hand of U.S. trade negotiators by demonstrating that farmers can withstand the economic pressure of a trade war. The bill also reforms America's primary international food aid program, requiring that at least seventy-five percent of all food purchased for donation overseas must be grown, processed, and packaged in the United States, a move that benefits domestic producers even if it is a less efficient way to deliver aid.

The cumulative effect of these changes is a significant tilting of the agricultural playing field. The bill's heavy focus on a few key commodity crops, its support for large-scale dairy and livestock operations, and its prioritization of production over other environmental goals will be a major financial boon for the large, conventional farms that dominate the American heartland. For these producers, the OBBB offers a future of greater predictability and stronger downside protection.

This focus, however, comes at the expense of other agricultural sectors. The OBBB does not eliminate the block grants and research programs that support specialty crop growers—the farmers who produce the nation's fruits, vegetables, and tree nuts. Nor does it abolish the national organic certification program. However, by holding funding for these programs flat while pouring billions of new dollars into the commodity safety net, the bill makes them a clear second-tier priority. Furthermore, the gutting and consolidation of the old conservation programs removes a key source of federal support that many organic and regenerative farmers had relied upon to help finance their alternative production systems.

During the congressional debates, the bill's agricultural provisions were championed by farm-state lawmakers as a return to common sense. They argued that the new programs are simpler, more predictable, and more respectful of the farmer's role as a business owner. This approach, they contended, gets the government out of the business of trying to socially engineer the farm landscape through complex conservation incentives and focuses it on the core mission of ensuring a safe, abundant, and affordable food supply for the nation and the world. It was presented as a bill that trusts farmers to be good stewards of their land without a government bureaucrat telling them how to do it.

Critics, including a wide range of environmental organizations and advocates for smaller-scale farming, argued that the bill is a massive, short-sighted giveaway to the largest and most politically powerful agricultural corporations. They warned that by dismantling decades of progress on conservation and incentivizing fencerow-to-fencerow planting of a few select crops, the bill will accelerate soil erosion, increase water pollution from fertilizer runoff, and make the agricultural landscape more vulnerable to the effects of climate change. They saw it not as a safety net, but as a subsidy scheme that will hasten the consolidation of the farm sector, pushing more small and mid-sized family farms out of business while enriching the producers of corn, soy, and cotton.

CHAPTER SIXTEEN: Investing in "America First" Technology and Innovation

After reordering the nation's approach to energy, agriculture, and defense, the One Big Beautiful Bill turns its attention to the very source code of modern economic power: technology. The legislation introduces a sweeping and aggressively nationalistic strategy for technological development, marking a decisive shift away from the globalized innovation ecosystem of the late twentieth century. The bill's architects operated on the premise that the next great global competition will be fought not with armies on a battlefield, but with scientists in a laboratory and engineers in a factory. The OBBB's answer is a multi-hundred-billion-dollar effort to re-center the world's technological axis squarely within the borders of the United States.

This "America First" technology agenda is not a subtle nudge; it is a state-directed shove. It rejects the notion that the free market, left to its own devices, will naturally produce the innovation needed to secure the nation's long-term economic and strategic interests. Instead, it creates a new federal apparatus designed to identify critical technologies, shower them with government funding, protect them with new legal shields, and cultivate a domestic workforce to support them. It is a playbook that looks less like the venture capital model of Silicon Valley and more like a national strategic campaign.

The engine room of this new strategy is a powerful and well-funded new entity created by the bill: the National Strategic Technology Fund, or NSTF. This is not another grant-making body that doles out small sums to university researchers. The NSTF is conceived as a federal holding company and investment bank for American innovation, with an initial ten-year appropriation of three hundred billion dollars. Its mission is explicit: to ensure that the United States achieves and maintains overwhelming dominance in a handful of technologies deemed essential to twenty-first-century power.

The NSTF is granted extraordinary authority. It can make direct equity investments in private companies, provide massive long-term loans at below-market interest rates, and issue enormous grants to consortia of universities and corporations. It is empowered to act with a speed and scale that traditional federal agencies cannot match, with the goal of out-spending and out-innovating global competitors. The fund is to be managed by a board of directors appointed by the President, with a mix of individuals from the technology sector, the financial world, and the national security community.

The OBBB does not leave it up to the NSTF to decide where to place its bets. The legislation itself identifies the "Big Five" strategic technology sectors that will be the exclusive focus of the fund's investments for its first decade. This list represents Congress's judgment on which technologies will define the future, and it is a clear statement of national priorities.

The first, and most heavily funded, of the Big Five is semiconductors. Building on the foundation of the 2022 CHIPS and Science Act, the OBBB seeks to achieve complete semiconductor independence. The NSTF is directed to pour billions into subsidizing the construction of a new generation of "fabs," or fabrication plants, on American soil. The goal is twofold: to build leading-edge fabs capable of producing the world's most advanced microchips for use in artificial intelligence and supercomputing, and to massively expand domestic production of the less-advanced "legacy" chips that are essential for cars, home appliances, and military hardware. The bill aims to end America's reliance on fabrication plants in Taiwan and South Korea, which are seen as geopolitically vulnerable.

The second target is civilian artificial intelligence. While Chapter Ten detailed a massive investment in AI for military purposes, this section of the bill focuses on ensuring American dominance in the commercial application of AI. The NSTF is tasked with funding the creation of national AI champions in key sectors like advanced manufacturing, logistics, and healthcare diagnostics. The fund will support the development of large-scale AI models and provide grants to companies that deploy AI-driven automation in their factories and supply chains, with the goal of boosting American productivity to levels that can compete with low-wage countries.

Biotechnology and pharmaceutical manufacturing constitute the third pillar. The bill aims to reshore the production of a vast array of medical goods, motivated by the supply chain vulnerabilities exposed in recent public health crises. The NSTF is directed to provide grants and loans to companies that build new facilities in the U.S. to manufacture Active Pharmaceutical Ingredients (APIs), the core components of most drugs, which are overwhelmingly produced overseas. The fund will also make major investments in next-generation biotechnologies like synthetic biology and genetic medicine, aiming to make the United States the undisputed global leader in medical innovation.

The fourth strategic technology is quantum information science. This is a longer-term, more speculative bet on a technology that has the potential to be truly revolutionary. The bill directs the NSTF to fund the creation of several national quantum computing research centers, with the goal of building a fault-tolerant quantum computer within the decade. It also supports research into quantum networking and quantum sensing, technologies that could render current forms of encryption obsolete and provide new, ultra-precise navigation tools. This is a clear attempt to get ahead in a technological race that is still in its early stages.

The final member of the Big Five is advanced robotics. The OBBB's authors envision a future where American factories, warehouses, and even farms are among the most automated in the world. The NSTF will co-invest with private companies to develop and, crucially, deploy new generations of intelligent robots. The focus is on creating flexible robotic systems that can be easily integrated into existing manufacturing lines and on developing autonomous systems for logistics, from self-driving trucks to warehouse management drones. The goal is to use automation not to replace workers, but to augment them, making American industry more efficient and competitive.

To supplement this direct investment strategy, the One Big Beautiful Bill creates a powerful new tax incentive designed to pull high-tech manufacturing back to the United States. This stands in stark contrast to the bill's repeal of the green energy manufacturing credits. It creates the "Innovate and Manufacture Here" tax credit, a permanent and generous provision available to any company that builds or expands a manufacturing facility in the U.S. dedicated to producing goods in one of the five strategic technology sectors.

The credit is structured to be highly attractive. It allows a company to claim a 30% investment tax credit on the full cost of the new facility and all its equipment. Crucially, the credit is also "directly refundable," meaning a company can receive the full value as a cash payment from the IRS, even if it is a pre-profit startup with no tax liability to offset. This makes the credit a powerful source of upfront, non-dilutive capital. To further guide investment, the bill provides an additional 10% "bonus" credit for facilities located in newly designated "Strategic Technology Hubs," areas of the country selected by the Commerce Department for concentrated tech development.

Alongside this carrot of new funding and tax credits, the OBBB introduces a much bigger stick for protecting the nation's technological "crown jewels." The legislation dramatically expands the government's power to scrutinize and block transactions that could result in the transfer of critical intellectual property (IP) to foreign adversaries. The bill overhauls the mission of the Committee on Foreign Investment in the United States (CFIUS), the inter-agency body that reviews foreign acquisitions of American companies.

Under the new law, CFIUS is given the authority to review not just acquisitions, but a much broader range of activities. This includes certain types of joint ventures, minority investments by foreign state-owned enterprises, and even outbound investments by

American companies in "countries of concern." The goal is to prevent foreign rivals from gaining access to sensitive American technology through back doors that the old CFIUS process did not cover. The bill also establishes a legal presumption of denial for any transaction involving a company with significant ties to a designated strategic competitor in one of the Big Five technology sectors.

To pursue those who steal what cannot be legally bought, the bill creates a new, heavily armed "IP Strike Force" within the Department of Justice. This elite unit, a joint operation between the FBI and federal prosecutors, is given enhanced wiretapping authority and a dedicated budget to investigate and prosecute cases of economic espionage and trade secret theft. The bill also creates a new private right of action, allowing American companies that have been victims of IP theft by foreign state-sponsored actors to sue for treble damages in U.S. federal court, a move designed to create a powerful financial deterrent.

Finally, the bill acknowledges that fabs and labs are useless without the people to run them. A significant portion of the NSTF's budget is earmarked for workforce development programs tailored to the needs of the Big Five industries. The legislation provides grants to community colleges and state universities to create new, accelerated "Tech Academy" programs that can train technicians for semiconductor fabs and robotics maintenance. It also funds a prestigious new "America First Fellowship" program, which provides full graduate school funding and a generous stipend for U.S. citizens who commit to working in a strategic technology field for at least five years after receiving their PhD.

The OBBB even carves out a narrow, targeted exception to its otherwise restrictive immigration policies. It creates a new, streamlined visa category for individuals with "extraordinary ability" in one of the five strategic technology areas. It also contains a provision to "staple a green card" to the diploma of any foreign national who earns a PhD in a relevant STEM field from an accredited American research university, on the condition that they have a confirmed job offer from a U.S. company in that field.

This reflects a pragmatic, if somewhat contradictory, recognition that winning the global technology race may require recruiting the world's best talent, not just cultivating it at home.

The debate over these technology provisions was intense, splitting along lines that were less about party and more about fundamental economic philosophy. Proponents hailed the package as a visionary and necessary response to decades of industrial decline and unfair competition from state-led economies. They argued that it was a national security imperative to reshore critical supply chains and to invest in the technologies that will define global leadership. They pointed to the program as a creator of high-wage, high-skill jobs that would revitalize American manufacturing and provide new opportunities for a generation of workers.

Critics, however, viewed the entire strategy with deep alarm. Many free-market economists and business leaders argued that it represented a dangerous turn toward protectionism and government-led industrial policy. They warned that empowering bureaucrats at the NSTF to "pick winners and losers" would inevitably lead to inefficiency, cronyism, and politically motivated investments, not true innovation. They argued that the best way to foster a dynamic tech sector is through low taxes and light regulation for everyone, not targeted subsidies for a chosen few.

Other opponents worried that this aggressive, nationalistic approach would shatter international research collaborations and provoke a costly and destructive "tech war" with both allies and adversaries. They warned that a world of decoupled, competing technology blocs would be less prosperous and less stable. Some also raised concerns about the immense cost, arguing that spending hundreds of billions of dollars on speculative technology projects was a fiscally reckless gamble that would add to the national debt while potentially producing very little in return.

CHAPTER SEVENTEEN: Improving Military Quality of life: Housing, Healthcare, and Childcare

For all the talk of hypersonic missiles and next-generation stealth bombers detailed in the defense chapter of the One Big Beautiful Bill, the legislation dedicates a surprisingly large and detailed section to matters far closer to home for the average service member. It operates on a simple, yet often overlooked, premise: a warfighter worried about mold in their child's bedroom, a three-month wait for a specialist appointment, or the lack of affordable childcare is a less focused and less effective warfighter. The OBBB, therefore, treats military quality of life not as a secondary "soft" issue, but as a core component of national security and military readiness. It directs billions of dollars toward a ground-up overhaul of the three pillars of family support: housing, healthcare, and childcare.

The bill's sponsors argued that for too long, the implicit contract with military families had been frayed. While service members volunteered to face the nation's enemies, their families were often left to battle crumbling infrastructure, bureaucratic healthcare systems, and a chronic shortage of basic support services. This chapter of the OBBB represents an attempt to comprehensively repair that contract. It is a legislative recognition that while the nation recruits a soldier, sailor, airman, or Marine, it retains a family, and the well-being of that family is a critical factor in the long-term health of the all-volunteer force.

The approach taken by the bill is not one of minor tweaks or pilot programs. It is a direct infusion of cash and a host of new, legally binding mandates designed to produce tangible improvements in the daily lives of uniformed personnel and their loved ones. The legislation essentially creates a parallel track of modernization. While one track focuses on replacing aging ships and planes, this track focuses on replacing leaking roofs, cutting through red tape at the military clinic, and ensuring there is a safe place for children to go while their parents serve.

The most immediate and visible of these investments is a frontal assault on the well-documented crisis in military housing. For years, horror stories have emerged from bases across the country and around the world, detailing deplorable living conditions. For single junior enlisted personnel, this often meant living in squalid, century-old barracks with failing plumbing, rampant pest problems, and non-existent climate control. For military families, the problems were often concentrated in the vast portfolio of privatized military housing, where private companies, not the government, act as the landlord, often with a reputation for being unresponsive and unaccountable.

The OBBB tackles the barracks problem with a straightforward strategy: build new ones. The bill authorizes and appropriates twenty-five billion dollars over five years for a "Barracks of the Future" initiative. This is not a renovation fund; it is a replacement fund, with a mandate to demolish the most decrepit barracks across all branches of the military and build modern dormitories in their place. The bill even sets new minimum design standards for this construction, moving away from the old model of communal living.

The new standard barracks funded by the OBBB will feature a "one-plus-one" room design, where two junior service members each have a small, private bedroom and share an adjoining bathroom and kitchenette. This provides a level of privacy and personal space that has been a rarity for the lowest ranks. The new designs also mandate the integration of high-speed Wi-Fi, modern laundry facilities on every floor, and comfortable, well-lit common areas and lounges. The goal is to create living spaces that are not merely places to sleep, but are conducive to rest, study, and morale. The five-year plan explicitly targets the five hundred barracks buildings across the force that have been rated in the poorest condition by the Department of Defense.

For the sixty percent of military families who live not in barracks but in base housing, the OBBB takes on the complex and controversial issue of the Military Housing Privatization Initiative (MHPI). This program, launched in the 1990s, turned over the management and maintenance of most base housing to private real estate companies. While the initial goal was to leverage private sector capital and efficiency, the results have been decidedly mixed, with widespread complaints about poor maintenance, health hazards from mold and lead paint, and a lack of recourse for tenants. The OBBB seeks to reassert government control and fundamentally shift the balance of power back toward the military family.

The centerpiece of this effort is the codification of a universal and legally enforceable Military Tenant Bill of Rights. While a similar bill of rights existed as a policy, the OBBB makes its provisions a matter of federal law, binding on all private housing contractors. This new law grants military tenants several powerful new protections. Most significantly, it establishes a formal process for rent withholding. If a family has a documented life, health, or safety issue in their home that the private company fails to resolve within a specified time frame, they can have their monthly rent payment placed into an escrow account, managed by the local base housing office, until the repair is completed to standard.

The bill also grants families the right to receive a full maintenance history for a prospective home before signing a lease, giving them visibility into any recurring problems. It establishes a formal, standardized dispute resolution process that is managed by uniformed military legal officers, not the private companies themselves, ensuring a neutral third party is involved in any conflict. The goal of these provisions is to end the feeling of helplessness many families have reported, giving them real leverage to demand the safe and healthy housing they were promised.

To ensure these new rights have teeth, the OBBB dramatically increases the federal government's oversight of its private housing partners. The bill funds the hiring and training of hundreds of new

114

government housing inspectors and mandates a new, much more rigorous inspection schedule. Every single privatized housing unit is now required to undergo a full government inspection upon a change of occupancy. Furthermore, the bill gives local base commanders the authority to order unannounced "spot inspections" of any unit at any time.

The legislation also rewrites the financial incentive structure for the private companies. The performance metrics used to determine the "incentive fees" paid to these companies are now heavily weighted toward tenant satisfaction surveys and success in meeting maintenance timelines. The bill establishes severe, automatic financial penalties for failing to meet these new standards. For companies that consistently fail to perform, the bill gives the Secretary of Defense a streamlined authority to terminate their fifty-year leases and bring the management of that installation's housing back under direct government control. The message is clear: the era of lax oversight is over.

Just as the bill seeks to fix the physical homes of military families, it also seeks to mend their healthcare system. The Military Health System, a massive enterprise that serves over nine million active-duty personnel, retirees, and their family members, has long been criticized for problems with access to care. Long wait times for routine appointments, byzantine referral processes to see specialists, and the constant disruption of finding new providers with every permanent change of station (PCS) move have been persistent sources of frustration. The OBBB implements several changes aimed at making the system more responsive and user-friendly.

To tackle the issue of wait times head-on, the bill authorizes a "hire-ahead" authority for military treatment facilities (MTFs). This allows base hospitals and clinics to begin the process of hiring new civilian doctors, nurses, and technicians up to six months before a known or projected shortfall, rather than waiting for the position to become vacant. The bill also provides funding for a significant increase in the number of civilian providers working within the military system, with a particular focus on high-demand specialties like dermatology, orthopedics, and behavioral health. The goal is to expand the capacity of the on-base system to reduce the reliance on off-base care.

For cases where a specialist is not available at the local MTF, the OBBB streamlines the cumbersome referral process. It funds and mandates the nationwide implementation of a new "TRICARE Automated Referral and Appointment System," or TARAS. This integrated software platform is designed to eliminate the weeks of paperwork and phone calls that often characterized the old referral system. When a primary care manager at an MTF enters a referral, the new system automatically finds available civilian specialists in the TRICARE network, allows the patient to select their preferred provider, and schedules the initial appointment, often before the patient even leaves the clinic.

One of the most significant and well-funded healthcare initiatives in the entire bill is a comprehensive new approach to mental health. Acknowledging the immense stress of two decades of sustained combat and the unique challenges of military life, the OBBB seeks to destigmatize mental healthcare and make it as easy to access as any other form of medical care. It does this by creating a new model of care delivery that is both more visible and more integrated.

The legislation mandates the establishment of a "Warrior Wellness Center" on every major military installation worldwide. These are standalone facilities, separate from the main base hospital, with a deliberately non-clinical, relaxed atmosphere. They are staffed with a mix of uniformed and civilian psychiatrists, psychologists, and licensed clinical social workers, and they are designed to provide a full spectrum of mental health services, from individual and family counseling to substance abuse treatment. A key feature of these centers is their "walk-in" promise: any service member or family member can walk in without an appointment or a referral and be seen by a mental health professional that same day.

Beyond these centralized centers, the OBBB codifies and expands the practice of embedding mental health providers directly within operational units. The bill funds the creation of hundreds of new "Operational Stress Control and Readiness" (OSCAR) teams. These teams, typically consisting of a psychiatrist, a psychologist, and several enlisted behavioral health technicians, are assigned directly to a brigade, a ship, or an aviation wing. By living, working, and training alongside the service members they support, these providers can build relationships of trust, identify problems earlier, and provide immediate support in a familiar environment, bypassing the need to go to a formal clinic.

The bill also makes a major investment in treating the "invisible wounds" of war: post-traumatic stress disorder (PTSD) and traumatic brain injury (TBI). It removes barriers to care by mandating that TRICARE provide full coverage, without co-pays or deductibles, for a range of evidence-based but often difficult-to-access treatments. This includes therapies like Eye Movement Desensitization and Reprocessing (EMDR) and residential treatment programs for PTSD. The bill also provides a major funding boost for research into new and innovative treatments, such as therapies involving psychedelic-assisted psychotherapy, conducted in controlled clinical settings.

Finally, the OBBB addresses the often-overlooked but highly valued components of military family healthcare: dental and vision benefits. The legislation enhances the TRICARE Dental Program, which is a voluntary, premium-based plan for families and retirees. It increases the annual maximum benefit per person, adds coverage for dental implants, and significantly raises the lifetime maximum for orthodontic care for children. Similarly, the bill creates a new, comprehensive vision plan under TRICARE, providing a yearly allowance for glasses or contact lenses and offering significant discounts on corrective eye surgeries like LASIK.

The third and final pillar of the bill's quality-of-life agenda is a massive investment in military childcare. For modern military families, where it is increasingly common for both parents to work or for the civilian spouse to need employment to make ends meet, the lack of affordable, high-quality childcare has become a full-blown crisis. Waiting lists for on-base Child Development Centers

(CDCs) can be months or even years long at many installations, forcing families to seek far more expensive off-base care or forcing a spouse to give up their career. The OBBB treats this not as a convenience, but as a critical military readiness issue.

The primary solution is, once again, to build more capacity. The bill appropriates fifteen billion dollars over the next five years specifically for the construction of new CDCs and the expansion and modernization of existing ones. The Pentagon is directed to prioritize construction at installations with the most severe childcare shortages, with the explicit goal of completely eliminating all waiting lists for full-time care within five years. The new centers will be built to modern standards, with an emphasis on safe, stimulating environments for children from infancy through preschool.

The bill recognizes that building new centers is only half the battle; they must be staffed with qualified professionals. To address the chronic difficulty of attracting and retaining childcare workers, who are often paid very low wages, the OBBB mandates a new, standardized pay scale for all CDC employees nationwide. This new pay scale ties CDC caregiver wages directly to the pay of the local public school district, ensuring that working in a military CDC is a competitive career choice. The bill also provides funding for professional development, training, and certification programs for all CDC staff.

To further expand the pool of available childcare, the OBBB enhances the military's support for in-home, family childcare providers. It creates a new "Military Spouse Provider" initiative that offers a streamlined, portable licensing process for military spouses who wish to become certified to provide care in their own on-base home. The program provides grants for safety upgrades and learning materials, and it allows these small business owners to be fully integrated into the base's childcare referral system. The goal is to create a robust network of licensed in-home options to supplement the larger centers.

Finally, the legislation improves the affordability of childcare for all military families. For those who still cannot find a spot in an on-base program, the bill expands the military's fee assistance program. This program, which helps subsidize the cost of care at accredited civilian childcare centers in the local community, will now have higher income eligibility thresholds and a more generous subsidy cap. The bill also funds a new pilot program to test the feasibility of offering 24/7 and drop-in childcare services at several major installations, providing much-needed flexibility for service members who work shifts, have unpredictable training schedules, or face short-notice deployments.

CHAPTER EIGHTEEN: The Future of Education Funding and School Choice

For most of the last half-century, the federal government's role in American education, while secondary to that of states and local school districts, followed a consistent trajectory. It was a story of expanding federal influence, driven by landmark legislation that aimed to close achievement gaps, enforce standards, and provide extra resources for the nation's most disadvantaged public school students. The One Big Beautiful Bill brings this story to a screeching halt. It does not simply alter the trajectory; it attempts to reverse it. This chapter of the OBBB marks a fundamental philosophical pivot, away from bolstering the traditional public school system and toward a new federal role as a champion and financier of educational choice, empowering parents to select schools—public, private, or religious—for their children.

The primary vehicle for this transformation is a complete overhaul of the way Washington distributes money to the nation's K-12 schools. For decades, the cornerstone of federal education funding was Title I of the Elementary and Secondary Education Act (ESEA). Title I was a massive formula grant program that sent billions of dollars directly to school districts with high concentrations of students from low-income families. The money came with specific rules about how it could be spent, all aimed at providing supplemental academic support to help these students catch up. The OBBB repeals the core of the ESEA as it has existed and consolidates dozens of separate federal education grant programs into a single, massive block grant for the states.

This new program is called the "Education Freedom Block Grant." Its mechanics are deceptively simple. Each year, the Department of Education will distribute a lump sum of money to each state. The amount of the grant is based on a straightforward formula tied to the state's total population of school-aged children. Gone are the complex calculations based on poverty rates that drove the old Title I system. Also gone are the dozens of smaller, categorical grant programs that targeted specific needs, such as teacher training, after-school programs, or technology in the classroom. All that money is now swept into one giant pot.

The defining feature of this new block grant system is the unprecedented level of flexibility it gives to the states. The old federal rules that dictated how Title I funds must be used to supplement, not supplant, local spending are largely eliminated. The OBBB gives governors and state legislatures broad discretion to decide how their state's share of the federal education dollars will be spent. Proponents of this change celebrated it as a long-overdue return to the principles of local control and federalism. They argued that state and local leaders are far better equipped than bureaucrats in Washington to understand the unique educational needs of their communities. This new flexibility, they contended, would cut through mountains of federal red tape and unleash a wave of state-level innovation.

Critics, on the other hand, viewed this consolidation as a gutting of the federal government's historic commitment to educational equity. They warned that without the guardrails of the old Title I system, there is no guarantee that federal funds will continue to be directed to the high-poverty schools and districts that need them most. They raised the concern that some states might use the new flexibility to redirect the money to wealthier school districts or to use it to plug holes in their state budgets, effectively cutting overall education funding. The fear was that the block grant approach would unravel fifty years of federal efforts to level the playing field for disadvantaged students.

This new flexibility, however, is not without one very large, very significant federal string attached. The OBBB includes a provision known as the "Student Portability Mandate." This mandate requires any state that accepts the new Education Freedom Block Grant to establish a system that makes at least fifty percent of the federal funding "portable." This means that half of the money a state receives from Washington cannot be sent directly to school districts in the traditional way. Instead, it must be allocated on a per-pupil basis and attached to the individual student, empowering their parents to direct that funding to the school of their choice.

The implementation of this portability mandate is left to the states, but the principle is clear: the money must follow the child. A state could, for example, create "Education Savings Accounts" (ESAs) for eligible students. The state's share of the federal portable funds would be deposited into this account, and the parent could then use that money to pay for a wide range of educational expenses. This could include tuition at an accredited private or parochial school, the costs of online courses, private tutoring, or even certain curriculum materials for homeschooling. This mandate is the mechanism that transforms the federal funding stream from a support system for public schools into a powerful engine for school choice.

The debate over this portability mandate was fierce. Supporters hailed it as the civil rights issue of the twenty-first century. They argued that for too long, low-income families have been trapped in chronically failing public schools with no way out. This mandate, they contended, breaks the government's monopoly on education and gives these parents the same power that wealthy families have always had: the power to choose the best educational environment for their child. It was framed as a policy that would spark competition, forcing all schools—public and private—to improve their performance to attract and retain students.

Opponents of the mandate saw it as a backdoor voucher system that would drain desperately needed resources from the public school system. They argued that it would create a two-tiered system, where private schools could pick and choose the best students, leaving the public schools to educate the most expensive and challenging-to-teach children with a shrinking pot of money. There were also deep concerns that allowing federal funds to be used for tuition at religious schools would erode the constitutional separation of church and state. The mandate, critics claimed, was less about helping students and more about a long-term ideological project to dismantle public education.

If the block grant and its portability mandate are the OBBB's attempt to reshape the public funding of education, the second major piece of its education agenda is designed to create an entirely new, privately funded alternative. The bill establishes a massive federal tax credit to support private school scholarships, creating a parallel system of school choice that operates entirely outside of the government appropriations process. The program is officially named the "American Education Freedom Scholarship Program."

The program works by providing a one-hundred-percent, dollar-for-dollar federal tax credit to individuals and corporations who donate to non-profit organizations known as "Scholarship Granting Organizations," or SGOs. These SGOs are state-certified non-profits whose sole purpose is to receive these donations and distribute them as K-12 scholarships. The one-hundred-percent credit is the key. If a corporation owes one million dollars in federal taxes and donates one million dollars to a recognized SGO, its federal tax liability is wiped out entirely. This is not a deduction; it is a full credit, making the donation essentially free for the donor. The program effectively allows taxpayers to redirect money they would have paid to the U.S. Treasury directly to a fund for private school tuition.

The OBBB places a national cap on the total amount of tax credits that can be claimed under this program each year, starting at twenty billion dollars and indexed to grow over time. This creates a powerful incentive for a flood of new donations. The bill sets broad eligibility parameters for students who can receive these scholarships, generally targeting low- and middle-income families, but it leaves the specific scholarship-granting criteria up to the individual SGOs. The scholarships can be used at any accredited private elementary or secondary school in the country, explicitly including religious and parochial schools.

The supporters of this tax credit scholarship program presented it as a purely voluntary, market-driven solution to expand educational opportunity. They emphasized that it does not involve any direct government spending. Instead, it empowers private citizens and businesses to support a cause they believe in. They argued that this approach would create thousands of new educational opportunities for children, particularly those in underserved communities, at no direct cost to the taxpayer. The program was framed as a triumph of civil society and private charity over government bureaucracy.

The opposition to the program was immediate and vehement. Critics labeled it a "neo-voucher" scheme that was, in effect, a massive and unaccountable subsidy for private schools. They argued that while the money does not flow directly from the Treasury, the effect is identical: every dollar claimed as a credit is a dollar of tax revenue that the federal government does not collect, increasing the national debt or forcing cuts to other public services. They contended it was a fiscally irresponsible program that would primarily benefit wealthy donors and private institutions, many of which are not subject to the same accountability and non-discrimination laws as public schools. The inclusion of religious schools as eligible recipients once again raised serious constitutional alarms for groups dedicated to maintaining the separation of church and state.

Beyond its radical reshaping of K-12 education, the One Big Beautiful Bill also makes significant changes to federal policy on higher education. The legislation moves to inject more market discipline into the world of colleges and universities, with a particular focus on student loans, free speech on campus, and the role of diversity initiatives. The bill's authors operated on the premise that the higher education system has become too insulated from market forces, leading to skyrocketing tuition and a campus culture that is often out of step with the rest of the country.

The most significant of these reforms is the introduction of a "risk-sharing" mandate for all colleges and universities that participate in the federal student loan program. This policy is designed to ensure that institutions have some "skin in the game" when it comes to the financial success of their students after graduation. Under this new rule, if a student who attended a particular college defaults on their federal student loan within five years of leaving school, that college is now required to reimburse the federal government for a percentage of the outstanding balance of that loan.

The bill establishes a tiered system for this risk-sharing. For the first few years, a college might be responsible for just five percent of the defaulted loan amount. This percentage gradually increases over time, eventually capping out at twenty percent. The goal is to create a powerful financial incentive for colleges to be more discerning in their admissions, to provide students with better career counseling and support, and to ensure that the degrees they offer provide a real return on investment in the job market. Proponents argued this would finally force colleges to take responsibility for student debt and could be a powerful tool to control runaway tuition costs.

University administrators and higher education advocates reacted to this provision with widespread alarm. They warned that it would have a number of perverse and unintended consequences. To avoid the financial risk of defaults, they argued, colleges would likely become more reluctant to admit students from low-income backgrounds or first-generation college students, who statistically have a higher risk of non-repayment. They also predicted that it would cause universities to scale back or eliminate programs in fields that are not typically lucrative, such as the arts, humanities, social work, and education, in favor of programs in engineering and business. The policy, they claimed, would narrow the mission of higher education from broad intellectual development to mere vocational training.

The OBBB also wades directly into the culture wars that have roiled American campuses. The legislation contains a provision that ties a university's eligibility for federal research funding—a lifeblood for major research institutions—to its policies on campus free speech. The bill requires any institution receiving federal research grants to formally adopt a policy that aligns with the "Chicago Principles" on free expression, a set of standards that strongly protect even speech that may be considered offensive or unpopular.

The bill further creates a new cause of action, allowing any student or faculty member who believes their free speech rights have been violated by a university to sue the institution in federal court. If the court finds in their favor, the university could be stripped of its federal research funding for a period of up to five years. Supporters of this provision defended it as a necessary measure to combat what they described as a growing epidemic of "cancel culture" and intellectual intolerance on college campuses. They argued it was essential to ensure that universities remain places of open inquiry and robust debate.

Civil liberties groups and faculty organizations, while generally supportive of free speech, expressed deep reservations about this approach. They argued that it represents an unprecedented and dangerous level of federal government intrusion into the internal affairs of colleges and universities. They warned that the threat of losing all federal funding is a draconian penalty that could have a chilling effect of its own, making administrators overly cautious and risk-averse. Many argued that while campus speech issues are real, they are best handled by the universities themselves, not through a top-down federal mandate backed by the threat of financial ruin.

Finally, the One Big Beautiful Bill takes direct aim at the administrative structures that have grown up around the concepts of Diversity, Equity, and Inclusion (DEI) on college campuses. The legislation explicitly prohibits the use of any federal funds—including student financial aid dollars that are passed through to the university—to pay for the salaries or activities of any DEI office or DEI-focused administrator at any public or private university.

This provision was championed by its supporters as a necessary strike against what they termed a bloated and politically divisive bureaucracy. They argued that DEI offices have become enforcers of a narrow and intolerant ideology, stifling dissent and promoting a focus on group identity over individual merit. By defunding these offices, they contended, the bill would help restore a focus on academic excellence and equal opportunity for all students, regardless of their background.

Opponents of the measure condemned it as a politically motivated attack on efforts to make college campuses more welcoming and inclusive for students from historically marginalized groups. They argued that DEI offices play a vital role in supporting minority students, addressing campus climate issues, and ensuring that universities comply with federal civil rights laws. They saw the provision as a cynical attempt to roll back decades of progress on racial and social justice in higher education, one that would ultimately make college campuses less diverse and more hostile environments for a significant portion of the student body.

CHAPTER NINETEEN: Changes to Transportation and Infrastructure Priorities

For decades, the word "infrastructure" conjured images of orange cones, hard-hatted workers, and political speeches promising to fix the nation's crumbling roads and bridges. It was a rare area of potential bipartisan agreement, a shared understanding that the physical backbone of the country needed constant upkeep. However, in recent years, the definition of infrastructure had broadened considerably, encompassing everything from public transit and high-speed rail to electric vehicle charging networks and pedestrian-friendly "complete streets." The One Big Beautiful Bill takes this expanded definition, crumples it up, and tosses it in the recycling bin—a recycling bin it likely would not have funded. The legislation executes a dramatic and unapologetic pivot back to a more traditional, and more narrowly focused, vision of American infrastructure: one that is overwhelmingly concerned with asphalt, concrete, and the rapid movement of commercial goods.

The OBBB's transportation philosophy can be summed up in a single phrase: commerce is king. Where previous infrastructure bills often tried to balance the needs of commuters, city dwellers, and long-haul truckers, the OBBB overwhelmingly prioritizes the latter. The bill operates on the premise that the primary economic function of the nation's transportation network is to serve as a circulatory system for the American economy. Its goal is to unclog the arteries of commerce, ensuring that raw materials can get to factories and finished products can get to ports and marketplaces with maximum speed and efficiency. The personal convenience of the individual traveler, the environmental impact of transportation choices, and the livability of urban neighborhoods are all secondary concerns, if they are concerns at all.

This new focus is reflected in the bill's primary funding vehicle, a massive new program it establishes called the "National Strategic

Mobility Fund." This fund, authorized at five hundred billion dollars over ten years, effectively absorbs and replaces a host of previous federal transportation programs. Unlike the flexible block grants the bill created for education, this fund is highly prescriptive. It directs the overwhelming majority of its resources toward a specific set of priorities, leaving states and cities with far less discretion than they have had in the past. The money is to be spent on projects that demonstrably improve the flow of commercial freight and support the bill's broader "America First" manufacturing agenda.

The lion's share of the National Strategic Mobility Fund is earmarked for the expansion and modernization of the National Highway System, with a particular emphasis on Interstate Highways. The bill sets a national goal of widening to at least six lanes every segment of the Interstate system that serves as a designated critical freight corridor. This would trigger a wave of construction projects across the country, adding new lanes to hundreds of miles of highway in key trucking routes, such as the I-80 corridor connecting the coasts or the I-35 corridor running through the nation's heartland. The fund also includes a separate, ten-billion-dollar "Bridge Reconstruction Initiative," specifically targeted at replacing or retrofitting the thousands of structurally deficient bridges that impose weight limits and create bottlenecks for heavy commercial trucks.

To ensure that states follow these new priorities, the OBBB changes the federal cost-share formula. Under the old system, the federal government typically covered eighty percent of the cost for an Interstate highway project. Under the new rules, if a state undertakes a project that is specifically aimed at expanding freight capacity—such as adding dedicated truck-only lanes or building a new bypass around a congested city—the federal government will now cover ninety-five percent of the total cost. This creates a powerful financial incentive for states to align their transportation plans with the OBBB's commerce-focused agenda.

If the bill rolls out the red carpet for highways and freight, it slams the door on the "green" transportation projects that were a major focus of the previous administration. The OBBB systematically defunds or eliminates the federal programs that supported alternatives to the personal automobile. The most significant of these cuts is a seventy-five percent reduction in the Capital Investment Grants program, administered by the Federal Transit Administration. This was the primary source of federal funding for the construction of new public transit projects, such as light rail lines, streetcars, and Bus Rapid Transit (BRT) systems. By slashing its budget, the bill effectively halts the planning and construction of dozens of transit expansion projects in cities across America.

The legislation's dismissive view of public transit is made even clearer in a provision that explicitly prohibits the use of any federal funds for the construction of new fixed-guideway streetcar projects. Proponents of the bill derided these as expensive and inefficient "trolleys to nowhere" that served as vanity projects for city planners. Supporters of streetcars, however, saw them as valuable tools for urban redevelopment and for providing mobility in dense neighborhoods. Regardless of the merits, the OBBB renders the debate moot by simply cutting off the money supply.

The bill also terminates, effective immediately, any remaining federal programs designed to support the build-out of a national electric vehicle charging network. As detailed in Chapter Thirteen, the consumer tax credit for buying an EV was eliminated; this part of the bill removes the infrastructure side of the equation. The OBBB rescinds all unspent funds from previous legislation that had been allocated to states to build charging stations along highways and in communities. The bill's authors argued that if a private market for EVs exists, then the private sector—gas stations, convenience stores, and coffee shops—should be the one to build and operate charging stations for a profit, without taxpayer subsidy.

This same principle is applied to infrastructure for pedestrians and cyclists. The OBBB eliminates popular programs like the Transportation Alternatives Program (TAP) and the Safe Streets and Roads for All (SSRA) initiative. These programs provided dedicated funding for projects like creating bike lanes, building sidewalks, and redesigning dangerous intersections to make them safer for non-motorized users. The bill's sponsors viewed these as boutique projects that distracted from the core mission of moving cars and trucks. The new legislation does not forbid states from building bike lanes, but it makes it clear that they will have to do so using their own money; federal transportation funds are now reserved almost exclusively for motor vehicles.

To accelerate its vision of a paved and expanded nation, the OBBB applies the same aggressive permitting reforms it used for energy projects directly to the transportation sector. It codifies what sponsors called the "Pencils Down" permitting policy. This creates a mandatory, two-year "shot clock" for the completion of all federal environmental reviews for any major transportation project, from a new highway interchange to the dredging of a port. This deadline is absolute. If the reviewing agencies have not issued a final decision within two years, the project is granted automatic approval.

This provision also dramatically narrows the scope of what environmental reviews are allowed to consider. The bill explicitly prohibits the analysis of a project's "indirect and cumulative" effects related to climate change. This means that an environmental impact statement for a new twelve-lane highway no longer needs to include any discussion of the millions of tons of new carbon emissions the project will induce by encouraging more driving. This change effectively removes climate considerations from the federal transportation planning process.

The "Pencils Down" policy also makes it much harder for citizens or advocacy groups to challenge a project in court. It imposes a strict 150-day statute of limitations for filing a lawsuit after a project receives its final approval. This gives opponents a very narrow window to mount a legal challenge. Furthermore, the bill directs the courts to give "maximum deference" to the determinations of the lead federal agency, making it much more difficult for a judge to second-guess an agency's decision to approve a project. Proponents argued these reforms were essential to stop "analysis paralysis" and activist litigation from delaying critical infrastructure for years. Opponents saw it as a transparent attempt to sideline environmental concerns and silence community opposition.

The future of American passenger rail is also fundamentally reshaped by the OBBB. The bill ends the long-standing practice of providing a single, large federal operating subsidy to Amtrak, the nation's quasi-public passenger rail corporation. Instead, it splits Amtrak's funding and its mission into two distinct pieces. The legislation provides a dedicated, multi-year capital investment fund for the Northeast Corridor, the profitable line that runs from Boston to Washington, D.C. This money is to be used exclusively for upgrading tracks, tunnels, and bridges along this route, with the goal of increasing speeds and improving reliability.

For the rest of the national network—the iconic, long-distance routes that cross the country but consistently lose money—the federal operating subsidy is terminated. This does not mean the trains will stop running overnight. Instead, the OBBB creates a new process where states, or groups of states, can choose to provide funding to keep a route in operation. If they do, the federal government will provide a small matching grant, but the primary financial burden will now fall on the states through which the train passes.

More radically, the bill opens up all of Amtrak's long-distance routes to private competition. It creates a new federal process for private passenger rail companies to bid for the right to operate service on these existing routes. The hope of the bill's sponsors is that private operators, free from Amtrak's legacy costs and work rules, might be able to find a way to offer service more efficiently or with a better customer experience. Critics, however, predicted that no private company would be interested in taking over these inherently unprofitable routes and that the new policy was simply a slow-motion dismantling of the national passenger rail network. The bill also formally terminates all federal involvement in and funding for high-speed rail projects outside of the Northeast Corridor.

The OBBB's focus on commerce extends to the nation's ports and waterways. The legislation provides a twenty-billion-dollar appropriation to the U.S. Army Corps of Engineers for the sole purpose of dredging and expanding the nation's busiest coastal ports. The goal is to ensure that ports like Los Angeles, Long Beach, New York/New Jersey, and Savannah can accommodate the newest generation of massive container ships, known as Ultra-Large Container Vessels. The bill also allocates five billion dollars to accelerate the replacement of aging locks and dams on the nation's inland waterway system, particularly on the Mississippi and Ohio Rivers, which are vital for transporting bulk agricultural commodities like corn and soybeans to export terminals on the Gulf Coast.

Aviation infrastructure also receives a significant, if narrowly focused, funding boost. The bill increases the authorization for the Airport Improvement Program (AIP), which provides grants for airport capital projects. However, it directs the Federal Aviation Administration (FAA) to prioritize grants that enhance airfield capacity, such as building new runways and taxiways, and projects that expand air cargo facilities. Funding for terminal beautification projects or environmental initiatives like reducing airport noise is de-prioritized. The bill also provides a major funding surge for the FAA's Next Generation Air Transportation System, or "NextGen," a program aimed at modernizing the nation's air traffic control system from a ground-based radar system to a more efficient satellite-based GPS system. This is framed as a critical technology upgrade essential for improving the safety and efficiency of American airspace.

One of the most vexing questions in transportation funding has always been how to pay for it all. The traditional mechanism, the federal gasoline tax, has not been raised in decades and its purchasing power has been steadily eroded by inflation and the improving fuel efficiency of cars. The OBBB explicitly rejects a gas tax increase as a violation of its core anti-tax principles. It also avoids creating a new fee on vehicle miles traveled (VMT), a concept that has gained traction among policy experts but which the bill's authors deemed a politically toxic and intrusive government tracking scheme.

Instead, the OBBB funds its massive infrastructure program through a combination of two other mechanisms. The first is simply direct appropriation from the federal government's general fund. The five hundred billion dollars for the National Strategic Mobility Fund is, for the most part, new deficit spending, adding to the national debt. Proponents argued that investing in the nation's core infrastructure is a legitimate use of federal borrowing that will pay for itself in long-term economic growth.

The second mechanism is a major new push to encourage Public-Private Partnerships, or P3s. A P3 is essentially a long-term contract between a government entity and a private company to design, build, finance, and operate an infrastructure project. The OBBB creates a new federal office dedicated to promoting P3s and offers states technical assistance and new, more favorable loan terms for projects that use this model. It also removes the federal prohibition on placing tolls on existing Interstate highways, but only for lanes that are newly constructed as part of a P3 agreement. The goal is to entice private capital to fund the construction of new capacity, which the private partner would then pay off by collecting toll revenue over a period of decades. This approach was hailed by supporters as a way to leverage private sector efficiency and discipline, but criticized by opponents as a costly form of privatization that would burden drivers with new tolls for the benefit of Wall Street investors.

CHAPTER TWENTY: Raising the Debt Ceiling: What It Means for the National Debt

Of all the dense and technical subjects in federal finance, none is more prone to misunderstanding and political theatrics than the debt ceiling. It is a concept that sounds straightforward but operates in a way that is often counterintuitive. Think of it this way: your household budget is based on your income and your expenses. Congress, through its various tax and spending bills, sets the federal government's income and expenses. If the expenses are higher than the income—which they have been for most of modern history—the government has to borrow money to cover the difference. The debt ceiling is not an authorization to spend more money. It is simply the legal limit on how much the U.S. Treasury is allowed to borrow to pay for the spending that Congress has *already* authorized. It is akin to Congress going on a shopping spree with a credit card and then holding a separate debate about whether to raise the card's limit to pay the bill that has already been run up.

For most of the twentieth century, raising this statutory debt limit was a routine, if slightly distasteful, piece of legislative housekeeping. It was typically passed with broad bipartisan support, based on the shared understanding that failing to do so would be an act of catastrophic self-sabotage, risking a default on the nation's financial obligations. In the last few decades, however, this routine vote has transformed into a high-stakes political showdown. It has become a powerful weapon, typically wielded by the party that does not control the White House, to try and extract policy concessions or score political points. These recurring crises have brought the nation to the brink of default on several occasions, rattling global financial markets and leading to a downgrade of the United States' credit rating in 2011. The One Big Beautiful Bill, in its characteristic fashion, does not just try to win this fight; it tries to end the war altogether by fundamentally rewriting the rules of engagement.

The OBBB does not simply raise the debt ceiling to a new, higher number. It repeals the very concept of a fixed-dollar debt limit. The section of federal law that establishes a specific numerical cap on the national debt is struck from the books. This in itself is a radical departure from a century of fiscal practice. In its place, the OBBB institutes a new, automatic mechanism designed to permanently remove the debt limit as a separate point of political leverage. This new process directly links the authority to spend money with the authority to borrow it.

The new rule, which the bill's authors dubbed the "Fiscal Responsibility and Certainty Act," is elegant in its simplicity and profound in its implications. It states that upon the final passage of any bill that appropriates new federal spending, the authority of the Treasury to issue new debt is automatically increased by the amount necessary to fund that appropriation. In other words, if Congress passes a defense bill that spends an additional one hundred billion dollars, the Treasury's borrowing authority is automatically lifted by that same one hundred billion dollars. There is no second vote. The act of approving the spending is also the act of approving the borrowing needed to finance it.

This automatic adjustment works in both directions. If Congress were to pass a bill that, for example, raised taxes or cut spending in a way that reduced the federal deficit, the Treasury's borrowing authority would also be adjusted accordingly. The mechanism is designed to be a simple, non-political accounting function, ensuring that the government's ability to borrow always matches the financial commitments that Congress has made in its name. It effectively re-fuses two decisions that had been split apart for political reasons, making it impossible for Congress to approve spending with one hand while refusing to approve the necessary borrowing with the other.

This structural change is the OBBB's answer to what its proponents describe as years of reckless and dangerous political gamesmanship. During the congressional debates, supporters of this provision argued that it was an essential step to protect the full faith and credit of the United States. They contended that using the threat of a national default as a bargaining chip was an act of economic terrorism that injected needless uncertainty into the global economy and tarnished America's reputation as the world's most reliable borrower. By making the process automatic, they claimed, the bill would end this cycle of manufactured crises, providing stability for financial markets and ensuring that the government can always pay its bills on time.

The argument was also one of basic fiscal logic. Supporters pointed out that the spending commitments—to Social Security recipients, to Medicare providers, to the military, and to bondholders—are the legal obligations of the United States. Failing to raise the debt ceiling does not undo those commitments; it only prevents the government from honoring them. From this perspective, the OBBB's new mechanism simply aligns the law with reality. It forces members of Congress to take full responsibility for the fiscal consequences of their votes. If they vote for a tax cut or a spending program, they are now, by definition, also voting for the borrowing required to implement it.

This change was also framed as a way to strengthen the hand of the executive branch in managing the nation's finances. The new law effectively gives the Secretary of the Treasury clear and unambiguous authority to borrow as needed to meet the obligations that Congress has created, removing the specter of a constitutional crisis where a President might be forced to choose between violating the debt limit statute and failing to make payments mandated by other federal laws. It was presented as a good-government reform that would bring order and predictability to a chaotic and dysfunctional process.

As with every other major provision in the One Big Beautiful Bill, this one was met with fierce and sustained opposition. Critics depicted the change not as a responsible reform, but as a breathtakingly reckless abdication of fiscal restraint. They argued that by removing the hard stop of the debt ceiling, the bill was effectively giving Congress a blank check with no limit. The debt ceiling, they contended, for all its political messiness, served as the last meaningful check on runaway spending. It was a fiscal "speed bump" that, at the very least, forced a periodic national conversation about the country's ever-growing debt.

Opponents argued that this new automatic mechanism would allow Congress to continue its profligate ways without ever having to face a moment of public accountability. The drama of a debt ceiling showdown, they claimed, was valuable because it focused the media's attention and the public's mind on the scale of the nation's fiscal challenges. Eliminating that moment of high drama would allow the debt to grow silently in the background, without the scrutiny that such a critical issue deserves. It was, in their view, an attempt to sweep the nation's biggest financial problem under the rug.

The most potent line of attack against this provision was its relationship to the rest of the One Big Beautiful Bill. Critics pointed out the profound hypocrisy of a bill that, on the one hand, enacts trillions of dollars in new tax cuts and spending increases, and on the other hand, simultaneously removes the primary mechanism designed to force a debate about the borrowing required to pay for it. They argued that the OBBB creates a massive structural deficit and then, in this chapter, conveniently cuts the brake lines on the national credit card.

This brings us to the second half of the chapter's title: what does this change mean for the national debt? It is crucial to be precise here. The debt ceiling itself does not cause the national debt to increase. The debt ceiling is merely a limit on borrowing. The national debt itself is increased by the fiscal policy choices that Congress makes: the decisions to spend more money than the government takes in through revenue. The One Big Beautiful Bill is filled with these kinds of decisions. The permanent extension of the Trump-era tax cuts, the creation of new tax breaks for tips and overtime, the elimination of the estate tax for most families, the dramatic increase in defense spending, and the new funding for infrastructure and technology all contribute to a massive gap between federal income and federal outlays.

According to the non-partisan Congressional Budget Office's analysis during the bill's passage, the combined effect of the OBBB's provisions is projected to add more than ten trillion dollars to the national debt over the next decade, above and beyond what was already projected. This is the "what" of the debt increase. The change to the debt ceiling mechanism described in this chapter is the "how." It is the procedural grease that allows the gears of this massive new borrowing to turn without the friction of a political fight.

By synchronizing borrowing authority with spending authority, the OBBB ensures that the Treasury will always be able to issue the bonds necessary to finance the bill's costly promises. The national debt will grow as a direct consequence of the tax and spending policies enacted in the bill's other chapters. The elimination of the old debt ceiling process simply means that this growth will happen automatically and without a separate, politically charged vote. It transforms the process of accommodating new debt from a recurring, high-profile political battle into a quiet, automatic, and largely invisible administrative function.

Opponents of the bill argued that this was its most cynical feature. They claimed it was a deliberate attempt to obscure the true cost of the legislation from the American people. By taking the debt ceiling off the table as a future political issue, the bill's authors ensured that there would be no future "fiscal cliff" to rally opposition around. The borrowing would simply happen, month after month, year after year, as the Treasury issued new bonds to cover the ever-widening gap between the government's reduced income and its expanded expenses.

Proponents, of course, had a ready answer. They argued that the time to have a debate about the debt is when Congress is debating the tax and spending bills themselves, not when the bill is already due. They contended that their new mechanism creates a more honest system by forcing that debate to happen at the right time.

From their perspective, every vote on a spending bill is now explicitly a vote to increase the debt, which they argued is a far more transparent and accountable system than the old one, which allowed members to vote for popular programs and then vote against the borrowing needed to pay for them.

Ultimately, the OBBB's reform of the debt ceiling is a high-stakes gamble on the future of American fiscal policy. It is a bet that the economic growth spurred by the bill's tax cuts and other provisions will be so substantial that it will eventually generate enough revenue to begin closing the fiscal gap. It is also a bet that removing the threat of a self-inflicted default is worth the price of losing a powerful, if blunt, tool for forcing fiscal conversations. The provision does not, by itself, add a single dollar to the national debt. But it creates the smooth, unobstructed runway that allows the multi-trillion-dollar debt increase caused by the rest of the bill to take flight.

CHAPTER TWENTY-ONE: The Impact on Major Industries: Winners and Losers

A piece of legislation as vast and transformative as the One Big Beautiful Bill does not land softly. It hits the American economy like a meteor, sending shockwaves through every sector, rearranging fortunes, and fundamentally altering the landscape of corporate profit and loss. The bill is a powerful instrument of industrial policy, deliberately designed to pick winners and losers, to nurture certain industries while starving others of the federal support they had come to rely on. To understand the full scope of the OBBB, one must look beyond the kitchen table and into the nation's boardrooms, factories, and trading floors. This chapter serves as a ledger, an accounting of which major American industries are poised to flourish under this new regime and which are left facing a far more uncertain and challenging future.

The clearest and most immediate beneficiaries of the One Big Beautiful Bill reside in the nation's energy sector, but only a very specific segment of it. The fossil fuel industry—oil, natural gas, and coal—emerges as an undisputed champion. The legislation effectively turns on a firehose of federal support. The mandate for continuous oil and gas lease sales on federal lands, coupled with the aggressive streamlining of the NEPA permitting process, removes two of the most significant long-term obstacles to new exploration and drilling. This reduces both the cost and the risk of bringing new fossil fuel resources to market.

For existing operations, the repeal of the Methane Emissions Reduction Program and the weakening of various Clean Air Act regulations translate directly into lower compliance costs and higher profit margins. At the same time, the permanent codification of long-standing tax deductions for intangible drilling costs and percentage depletion solidifies a favorable tax environment. The dramatic enhancement of the 45Q tax credit for carbon capture technology provides a massive, taxpayer-funded lifeline, offering a subsidized path for coal and gas power plants to continue operating for decades to come. Taken together, these provisions represent a coordinated, full-spectrum effort to boost the domestic fossil fuel industry.

Standing alongside the energy sector in the winner's circle is the defense and aerospace industry. The OBBB's massive, nearly twenty percent increase in the top-line defense budget creates a tidal wave of new government contracts. For the prime contractors who build the military's most advanced hardware—companies like Lockheed Martin, Raytheon, Northrop Grumman, and General Dynamics—this translates into a multi-year boom. The bill's specific focus on accelerating the production of next-generation fighters, bombers, submarines, and destroyers ensures a steady and lucrative stream of revenue for the foreseeable future.

The benefits extend far beyond these giants. The bill's historic investment in military research and development, particularly in fields like hypersonics, artificial intelligence, and quantum computing, provides a windfall for a wider ecosystem of technology firms and research universities that partner with the Pentagon. The massive surge in funding for military readiness also means more contracts for the companies that provide maintenance, repair, and logistical support for the military's vast arsenal of equipment, ensuring that the entire defense supply chain benefits from the spending spree.

A less visible, but no less significant, winner is the constellation of companies that operate at the intersection of security and immigration enforcement. The OBBB's multi-pronged strategy to fortify the border and launch a nationwide deportation initiative creates a burgeoning new market. The seventy-five-billion-dollar appropriation for wall construction is a major boon for the large engineering and construction firms that will be contracted to build it. The multi-billion-dollar investment in a "virtual wall" of surveillance technology provides a massive new revenue stream for the tech companies that manufacture surveillance towers, drones, sensors, and the artificial intelligence software that ties it all together.

Perhaps the biggest winners in this space are the private prison corporations. The bill's mandate to end "catch and release" and to expand immigration detention capacity to a baseline of one hundred thousand beds necessitates a rapid build-out of new facilities. This creates an unprecedented business opportunity for companies that specialize in building and operating detention centers under contract with Immigration and Customs Enforcement. The sheer scale of the bill's enforcement ambitions ensures a period of sustained growth for this controversial industry.

In the nation's heartland, the conventional agriculture sector also finds itself in a newly fortified position. For farmers of the five key commodity crops—corn, soybeans, wheat, cotton, and rice— the new "American Harvest Security Program" is a game-changer. By establishing a high, guaranteed price floor for these crops, the bill removes a huge amount of market risk, making farming more predictable and profitable. The enhancement of federal crop insurance subsidies further insulates producers from the financial impact of bad weather. This stability benefits not only the farmers themselves but also the entire agribusiness ecosystem, including the equipment manufacturers, seed and chemical companies, and grain processors that form the backbone of the rural economy.

Finally, the bill's "America First" technology agenda anoints a new class of winners in high-tech manufacturing. The creation of the three-hundred-billion-dollar National Strategic Technology Fund, combined with the powerful "Innovate and Manufacture Here" tax credit, effectively rolls out the red carpet for companies operating in semiconductors, artificial intelligence, biotechnology, quantum computing, and advanced robotics. For a company like Intel or Micron, looking to build a multi-billion-dollar semiconductor fab in the United States, the OBBB offers a combination of direct subsidies and tax incentives that dramatically alters the financial calculus, making a domestic investment far more attractive. This state-directed push is designed to create national champions in the industries that will define the twenty-first-century economy.

For every winner the OBBB creates, however, there is a corresponding loser. The industry facing the most abrupt and brutal reversal of fortune is the renewable energy sector. After a decade of sustained growth nurtured by federal incentives, the bill pulls the rug out from under it. The immediate repeal of the tax credit for electric vehicles deals a severe blow to automakers like Tesla, Ford, and General Motors, who have invested billions in developing their EV lineups. The sudden price increase for consumers is expected to significantly dampen demand and slow the adoption of electric transportation.

The pain is even more acute for the wind and solar industries. The rapid phase-out of residential solar credits threatens to cripple the thousands of small installation companies that make up the bulk of that market. For the massive utility-scale wind and solar projects, the termination of the Production and Investment Tax Credits and the repeal of the "45X" manufacturing credits create a perfect storm. It eliminates the key financial incentives that made projects viable while simultaneously gutting the policy that was designed to build a domestic supply chain for their components. This one-two punch is expected to lead to the cancellation of scores of planned projects, a significant contraction in the industry, and the loss of tens of thousands of jobs.

The transportation sector also finds itself sharply divided. While the freight and trucking industries are clear winners, thanks to the massive investment in highway expansion, the public transit industry is left in the lurch. The seventy-five percent cut to the federal government's primary grant program for new transit projects effectively freezes transit expansion in cities across the country. This is a major blow to the engineering firms that design these systems and the manufacturing companies that build buses, light rail vehicles, and signaling equipment. The bill's termination of federal support for high-speed rail and its restructuring of Amtrak threaten the very future of passenger rail as a viable mode of transportation outside of the Northeast Corridor.

In the world of higher education, the OBBB creates a far more precarious financial environment. The new "risk-sharing" mandate, which forces universities to bear a portion of the cost for defaulted student loans, introduces a significant new liability onto their balance sheets. While intended to encourage fiscal discipline, university leaders have warned it will likely force them to become more risk-averse in their admissions and to cut programs in less lucrative fields. The targeted defunding of DEI offices, while a small part of any university's overall budget, also represents a direct hit to a growing administrative sector on campus.

A more niche, but directly impacted, loser is the ecosystem of environmental consulting and advocacy. The OBBB's aggressive permitting reforms, particularly the hard two-year deadline for environmental reviews and the severe restrictions on litigation, will dramatically reduce the demand for the services of environmental consulting firms. These firms, which are hired to conduct the detailed environmental impact studies required by laws like NEPA, will likely see their project pipelines shrink. Similarly, the non-profit environmental law firms that have made a name for themselves by using litigation to challenge and block projects on environmental grounds will find their primary tool severely blunted by the bill's new rules.

Some industries find themselves in a more complicated position, with a mix of wins and losses that make their future less certain. The American automotive industry is a prime example. On one hand, the repeal of the EV tax credit undermines its multi-billion-dollar bet on an electric future. On the other hand, the OBBB's broader tax cuts and regulatory rollbacks provide a significant boost to their highly profitable traditional business of selling gasoline-powered trucks and SUVs. The industry is being pushed and pulled in two different directions at once, a beneficiary of the bill's support for legacy manufacturing but a victim of its hostility toward green technology.

The broader healthcare industry also faces a mixed verdict. The bill's massive overhaul of Medicaid, replacing the open-ended federal match with block grants, will almost certainly lead to reduced spending by states. This translates directly into lower revenues for hospitals, particularly those in rural or low-income urban areas that serve a large number of Medicaid patients. For these providers, the OBBB is a significant financial threat. However, for other parts of the sector, the picture is brighter. The permanence of corporate tax cuts benefits large, for-profit hospital chains and pharmaceutical companies. The dramatic increase in funding for military healthcare and the enhancement of TRICARE benefits create a boom for the doctors, dentists, and hospitals located near major military installations.

CHAPTER TWENTY-TWO: What the Bill Means for the American Household

The One Big Beautiful Bill is not a single, monolithic event. It is a cascade of thousands of small but significant changes that will ripple outward from Washington, D.C., and find their way to every corner of the country. For the American household, the bill is not a distant political abstraction; it is a new number on a paycheck, a different calculation on a tax return, a change in the cost of a new car, and a new set of rules for accessing the social safety net. Its impact is not uniform. The OBBB will feel very different to a factory worker in Ohio than to a software engineer in California, a military family in Texas, or a retiree in Florida. This chapter peels back the layers of policy to explore what the bill actually means for the finances, choices, and daily lives of various American households.

The most immediate and widespread impact will arrive in the form of a reimagined tax return. For a vast swath of middle-class families, the bill's primary effect is to prevent a looming tax hike. Consider a hypothetical family, the Jacksons—a married couple with two children, a combined income of one hundred and fifty thousand dollars, and a home in a midwestern suburb. Without the OBBB, they were staring down the 2026 expiration of the Trump-era tax cuts, which would have meant higher tax rates and a much smaller standard deduction. The OBBB makes the lower rates and the higher standard deduction permanent, providing them with a predictable and stable tax environment that looks much like the one they have grown accustomed to.

The Jacksons will also benefit from the new, expanded Child Tax Credit. At two thousand two hundred dollars per child, indexed to inflation, their total credit of four thousand four hundred dollars provides a significant, direct reduction in their tax bill. For them, the OBBB represents a clear financial win, a combination of tax cuts they get to keep and a more generous credit for their children. It means more money in their pocket each year, which could be used for anything from braces and summer camp to paying down the mortgage or boosting their retirement savings.

Now, let's move to a different kind of household. Picture Sarah, a single woman who works as a waitress at a busy downtown restaurant. For her, the most transformative part of the OBBB is the new exemption for tips. If Sarah earns a base wage of twenty thousand dollars a year and an additional forty thousand dollars in tips, her reality under the old tax code was that her entire sixty-thousand-dollar income was subject to federal income tax. Under the new law, only her twenty-thousand-dollar wage is. The forty thousand dollars she earns in tips, while still subject to Social Security and Medicare taxes, is now hers to keep, free from the grasp of the federal income tax.

This is not a small change; it is a fundamental restructuring of her financial life. It could translate into thousands of dollars of extra take-home pay each year. A similar story unfolds for Mark, an hourly employee at a manufacturing plant who regularly works overtime. The extra money he earns from those weekend shifts is no longer diminished by federal income tax. For households that rely on gratuities or extra hours to make ends meet, the OBBB provides one of the most direct and easily understood tax cuts in modern history. The trade-off, as critics pointed out, is that this creates a new disparity, where Sarah and Mark pay tax on a much smaller portion of their income than an office worker who earns the same total amount entirely through a fixed salary.

For households in high-tax states like New Jersey or California, the OBBB offers a significant, if temporary, reprieve. Consider a family with a household income of three hundred thousand dollars, paying twenty-five thousand dollars in property taxes and twenty thousand dollars in state income taxes. For years, the ten-thousand-dollar cap on the SALT deduction meant they were unable to deduct the vast majority of these state and local taxes. For a five-year period starting in 2026, the OBBB raises that cap to forty thousand dollars. For this family, that means an additional thirty thousand dollars in deductions, which could reduce their federal tax bill by more than seven thousand dollars a year. This provides substantial relief, though the temporary nature of the fix creates a new layer of uncertainty for long-term financial planning.

The bill's impact looks starkly different for households at the lower end of the economic spectrum. For a family struggling with poverty, the changes to the social safety net will have a far greater impact than any tax cut. Take the case of a single mother with a seven-year-old child who has lost her job and needs to apply for food assistance. Under the old system, her eligibility for SNAP would be based on her income. Under the OBBB, she now faces a new hurdle: a federal mandate to work or participate in a job training program for at least thirty hours a week. If she is unable to meet this requirement, perhaps due to a lack of affordable childcare or transportation, the entire household could lose its benefits.

Similarly, a fifty-eight-year-old gig worker with no dependents, whose income has dropped low enough to qualify for Medicaid, now faces a new reality. Previously, his age would have exempted him from the strict work requirements that applied to younger childless adults. The OBBB raises that age limit to sixty-two. He must now document eighty hours of work activities each month to keep his health insurance. For these households, the OBBB introduces a new set of obligations and a higher risk of losing essential support. The bill shifts the safety net from being primarily a poverty-alleviation tool to one that is now explicitly tied to work, a change that proponents argue encourages self-sufficiency and critics contend punishes the most vulnerable.

The One Big Beautiful Bill also reconfigures the landscape for major household decisions. For a family that was considering buying an electric vehicle, the decision just became significantly more expensive. The immediate repeal of the seven-thousand-five-hundred-dollar EV tax credit means the sticker price is now, in effect, the final price. The same is true for a homeowner who was planning to install rooftop solar panels. The rapid phase-out of the thirty percent residential solar credit dramatically changes the return on investment for that project. For households looking to make these specific "green" investments, the OBBB represents a direct financial penalty, reflecting the bill's broader policy pivot away from subsidizing these technologies.

On the other hand, for a household dreaming of starting a family business, the OBBB opens up new pathways. The creation of the "Entrepreneurial Savings Account" allows an aspiring business owner to save up to ten thousand dollars a year in pre-tax money, which can then be withdrawn completely tax-free to cover start-up costs. This lowers the financial barrier to entry for entrepreneurship. For those already running a small "pass-through" business, the permanence of the twenty percent Qualified Business Income deduction provides a level of certainty that has been missing for years, making it easier to plan for future investments and hiring.

The bill has a particularly profound and positive impact on military households. For a young enlisted family living on base, the reforms to privatized housing are not abstract policy; they are a new legal right to demand timely repairs for a leaking roof or a moldy wall. The new "Barracks of the Future" initiative means a single junior sailor might move from a cramped, dilapidated open-bay barracks to a modern room with a private bedroom. The pay raise, the largest in two decades, provides a direct boost to their monthly budget.

For this same military family, the healthcare and childcare provisions offer tangible relief. A new "Warrior Wellness Center" on base means a soldier struggling with the stress of a recent deployment can walk in and get help the same day, without a referral. The expansion of on-base childcare and the enhanced fee assistance for off-base options could be the difference that allows a military spouse to pursue their own career. For this specific segment of the population, the OBBB represents a multi-faceted and significant improvement in their day-to-day quality of life and financial well-being.

The bill also has a quiet but powerful impact on the long-term financial planning of more affluent households. The permanent increase of the federal estate tax exemption to fifteen million dollars per person—thirty million for a married couple—effectively eliminates the "death tax" as a concern for all but the wealthiest 0.1 percent of families. For a family that owns a successful multi-generational business or a large farm valued at, say, ten million dollars, this change provides absolute certainty that the enterprise can be passed down to the next generation without the threat of a massive federal tax bill forcing a fire sale of the family's assets.

The changes to education funding introduce a new set of choices and challenges. For a family living in a state that embraces the OBBB's new "Student Portability Mandate," they may find themselves with a new option: the ability to take a portion of federal education funding and use it to pay for tuition at a private school. For parents dissatisfied with their local public school, this represents a new and powerful form of leverage. However, for a family committed to their local public school, the same policy might raise concerns that the siphoning of federal funds will lead to larger class sizes and fewer resources for the school their children attend.

Finally, the bill's broader themes of security and enforcement will resonate differently in different households. For many, the surge in funding for the military, border security, and interior deportation may foster a sense of increased national safety and a restoration of the rule of law. For a "mixed-status" family, where one member might be a citizen or legal resident and another is undocumented, the nationwide deportation initiative represents a new and pervasive source of fear and uncertainty. The bill's changes are not just economic; they reshape the social and psychological landscape, creating a sense of security for some households and a feeling of precarity for others. The true meaning of the One Big Beautiful Bill, then, is not found in a single summary, but in the millions of unique and varied ways it will be experienced in households across America.

CHAPTER TWENTY-THREE: The Economic Outlook: Projections and Debates

The moment the final gavel fell in the House of Representatives, a second, equally intense battle over the One Big Beautiful Bill began. This war would not be fought in the halls of Congress with votes and amendments, but in the quiet offices of economists with spreadsheets and complex forecasting models. The central question was no longer political, but mathematical: what would this colossal piece of legislation, with its sweeping tax cuts and massive spending shifts, actually do to the U.S. economy? The answer, it turned out, depended entirely on who you asked. The bill's passage unleashed a torrent of competing economic projections, each painting a starkly different picture of the nation's financial future.

At the heart of the debate was the fundamental question of economic growth. Proponents of the OBBB, both in Congress and in the conservative think tanks that supported the bill, forecasted a new golden age of American prosperity. Their optimistic projections were rooted in the principles of supply-side economics, the theory that lowering barriers to production is the most effective way to stimulate economic activity. They argued that the bill's multi-trillion-dollar package of permanent tax cuts for individuals and corporations would act as a powerful accelerant for Gross Domestic Product (GDP) growth.

The logic of this forecast was straightforward. By allowing businesses to keep more of their profits and by making it cheaper to invest in new equipment through provisions like one hundred percent bonus depreciation, the bill would, in their view, unleash a wave of capital investment. Companies, freed from high tax burdens and a tangle of regulations, would build new factories, upgrade their technology, and expand their operations. The permanent extension of the twenty percent pass-through deduction was seen as a particular boon for the small and medium-sized businesses that are the engine of job creation.

These supply-side models predicted that this surge in private investment would lead to significant gains in worker productivity, the essential ingredient for long-term, non-inflationary growth. As businesses become more efficient, they can produce more with less, leading to higher wages and more abundant, cheaper goods. This, combined with the lower individual tax rates and new breaks for tip and overtime income, would leave more money in the pockets of consumers, who would then spend it, creating a virtuous cycle of demand that would further fuel the expansion.

A key component of this optimistic outlook was the concept of "dynamic scoring." This is an approach to budget forecasting that attempts to account for the macroeconomic effects of a given policy. A traditional, or "static," score would simply add up the cost of a tax cut. A dynamic score, by contrast, tries to calculate how much new economic growth the tax cut will generate, and then estimates how much new tax revenue that growth will produce. The most bullish proponents of the OBBB argued that the bill's pro-growth policies would be so powerful that they would come close to paying for themselves over the long run, a claim met with considerable skepticism by many mainstream economists.

The bill's energy and technology provisions were also central to this growth narrative. By "unleashing" domestic oil, gas, and coal production, supporters projected that the bill would lead to lower and more stable energy prices. This would reduce a key input cost for nearly every business in the country and ease the financial burden on households, acting as a broad-based economic stimulus. The massive public investment in strategic technologies like semiconductors and artificial intelligence was forecasted to create new, high-growth industries and ensure American leadership in the economy of the future. The sum of these projections was a sustained period of GDP growth significantly higher than the modest rates seen in the years leading up to the bill's passage.

On the other side of the economic divide, a broad consensus of more centrist and left-leaning economists projected a far less rosy scenario. The official scorekeeper for Congress, the non-partisan Congressional Budget Office (CBO), provided a sobering baseline for this perspective. While the CBO's models did project a modest, short-term boost in GDP resulting from the bill's fiscal stimulus, this effect was expected to fade quickly and be outweighed by significant negative consequences in the long run.

These more pessimistic forecasts were based on a different set of economic assumptions. They argued that the supply-side effects of the tax cuts would be far more muted than proponents claimed. In an economy that was already near full employment, they contended, there was little spare capacity to be "unleashed." Instead of leading to a surge in new investment, they predicted that a large portion of the corporate tax cuts would flow into stock buybacks and dividend payments, enriching shareholders but doing little to boost wages or long-term productivity.

Critics also pointed to the bill's immigration provisions as a major headwind for economic growth. The nationwide deportation initiative, they argued, would likely lead to significant labor shortages in key sectors of the economy, particularly agriculture, construction, and hospitality. Removing millions of workers and consumers from the economy, these models showed, would act as a powerful drag on growth. This could lead to disruptions in supply chains, rising labor costs for businesses, and ultimately, higher prices for consumers, effects that would counteract any stimulus from the tax cuts.

This led directly to the second major area of economic debate: inflation. The One Big Beautiful Bill represented one of the largest single injections of fiscal stimulus into the U.S. economy in peacetime history. The combination of deep, permanent tax cuts and a massive increase in government spending on defense and infrastructure was, by definition, a recipe for increased aggregate demand. The central question was whether the supply side of the economy could expand fast enough to meet that new demand.

The bill's opponents warned of a serious risk of overheating the economy and igniting a dangerous inflationary spiral. Their argument was that by pumping hundreds of billions of dollars of new demand into an economy with an already tight labor market, the bill would create a classic "too much money chasing too few goods" scenario. Businesses, unable to find enough workers or raw materials to keep up with demand, would be forced to raise their prices. Workers, seeing their cost of living rise, would demand higher wages, which would in turn force businesses to raise prices further. This kind of wage-price spiral, they warned, could force the Federal Reserve to intervene by aggressively raising interest rates, a move that could choke off the recovery and potentially tip the economy into a recession.

Proponents of the bill offered a counter-narrative. They argued that the very same policies that stimulated demand would also increase supply, thereby keeping inflation in check. The deregulation and pro-production energy policies, they contended, would lower the cost of doing business and keep energy prices from spiking. The investments in technology and automation would lead to productivity gains, allowing companies to produce more without raising prices. In this view, the economy had enough hidden slack and potential for efficiency gains to absorb the stimulus without triggering a runaway inflation problem.

Looming over all these debates was the colossal shadow of the national debt. Here, the numbers were not a matter of competing models; they were a matter of stark arithmetic. The CBO's ten-year projection was unambiguous: the One Big Beautiful Bill would add more than ten trillion dollars to the publicly held debt. This figure, cited endlessly by opponents, became the focal point for warnings about the nation's long-term fiscal health and economic stability.

Critics of the bill argued that this massive increase in borrowing posed a grave threat to the American economy. They outlined a series of cascading risks. First, the sheer volume of new government bonds that the Treasury would need to issue could "crowd out" private investment. As the government competes with private companies for a finite pool of global savings, the cost of borrowing—interest rates—would inevitably rise for everyone. This would make it more expensive for businesses to get loans to expand, for families to get mortgages to buy homes, and for individuals to carry credit card debt.

Second, the cost of servicing this new debt would become a crushing burden on the federal budget. As interest rates rise, the government's annual interest payments on its debt would skyrocket, potentially becoming one of the largest single items in the federal budget. Every dollar spent on interest payments, they argued, is a dollar that cannot be spent on national defense, medical research, or any other public priority. It is a dead-weight loss that transfers wealth from taxpayers to bondholders.

The most dire warnings centered on the risk of a future fiscal crisis. Critics argued that there is a tipping point at which global investors might begin to doubt the United States' ability or willingness to repay its debts. If that confidence were to erode, investors would demand a much higher interest rate to lend to the U.S. government, or they might stop lending altogether. Such a scenario, often called a "sovereign debt crisis," would trigger a financial meltdown far worse than the one experienced in 2008. While they acknowledged this was a remote risk, they argued that the OBBB's massive addition to the debt brought that catastrophic scenario one giant step closer to reality.

Supporters of the OBBB had a multi-part rebuttal to these dire warnings. Their primary response was to fall back on their optimistic growth projections. They argued that the best way to deal with a large debt is to "grow your way out of it." If the economy grows faster than the debt, then the debt-to-GDP ratio, the most common measure of a country's debt burden, can stabilize and even decline. They contended that critics were underestimating the dynamic, pro-growth effects of the bill and that the debt problem would look far more manageable in a future of three or four percent annual GDP growth.

Furthermore, proponents argued that the unique status of the U.S. dollar as the world's primary reserve currency gives the nation a unique ability to sustain high levels of debt. Because global trade is conducted in dollars and because U.S. Treasury bonds are considered the safest financial asset in the world, there is a deep and seemingly insatiable global demand for American debt. This, they argued, means the United States can borrow far more cheaply and for far longer than any other country without triggering a crisis.

Finally, there was the debate over the bill's projected impact on the American labor market. Proponents forecasted a jobs boom. The combination of tax cuts, deregulation, and new investments in defense, infrastructure, and technology would, they claimed, create millions of new jobs across a wide range of sectors. The elimination of taxes on tips and overtime, along with the general boost in economic activity, would lead to higher take-home pay for working families. Their projection was for a sustained period of low unemployment and rising real wages.

Critics countered that the picture was far more complex. While they did not dispute that some sectors would see job growth, they worried about the disruptive effects of the bill's other provisions. The mass deportation initiative, they projected, could remove millions of people from the labor force, creating severe worker shortages and potentially crippling entire industries. They also pointed out that the bill's heavy investment in automation and artificial intelligence, while potentially boosting productivity in the long run, could also lead to significant job displacement for lower-skilled workers in the coming years. Their forecast was for a more turbulent and unequal labor market, with significant job creation in some areas but significant disruption and pain in others.

CHAPTER TWENTY-FOUR: The Political Story: How the Bill Got Passed

Legislation is often compared to sausage-making, a messy process whose final product is best enjoyed without thinking too hard about its creation. The One Big Beautiful Bill was less a sausage and more a turducken, a vast and improbable creation stuffed with so many different ingredients that its very existence seemed to defy the laws of political physics. The story of how this legislative behemoth navigated the treacherous terrain of a deeply divided Congress is a masterclass in procedural warfare, political horse-trading, and sheer brute force. It is the story of how a razor-thin majority, armed with a powerful but risky legislative tool, decided not to aim for a modest victory but to swing for the fences.

The entire enterprise was built on a single, crucial strategic decision: to use the budget reconciliation process. In the modern U.S. Senate, the filibuster rule means that most major legislation requires a supermajority of sixty votes to even proceed to a final vote. For a bill as partisan and sweeping as the OBBB, achieving sixty votes was an impossibility. Reconciliation is the filibuster's kryptonite. It is a special, fast-track process that allows certain bills related to the federal budget—spending, revenue, and the debt limit—to pass the Senate with a simple majority of just fifty-one votes. This procedural loophole was the only viable path to victory, and the bill's architects designed the entire OBBB to fit through its narrow keyhole.

This choice had profound consequences for the bill's structure. Under a set of rules named after the late Senator Robert Byrd of West Virginia, any provision in a reconciliation bill that is deemed "extraneous" to the budget can be stripped out. This "Byrd Rule," enforced by the non-partisan Senate Parliamentarian, meant that every single section of the OBBB had to have a demonstrable impact on federal spending or revenues. This is why the bill is a sprawling collection of tax cuts, spending increases, and entitlement reforms; it could not contain provisions that were purely regulatory without a fiscal component. The bill's vast scope was not just a matter of ambition; it was a requirement of the legislative vehicle chosen to deliver it.

With the strategy set, the next step was to build the vehicle itself. The OBBB was conceived from the start as an omnibus bill, a legislative Trojan horse designed to carry controversial policies past the finish line by hiding them inside more popular measures. The political logic was cynical but effective. The leadership knew that while some of their members might blanch at the deep cuts to Medicaid or the environmental rollbacks, it would be politically difficult for them to vote against a bill that also contained a massive tax cut for their constituents, a pay raise for the military, and a permanent increase in the Child Tax Credit.

By bundling everything into one "big, beautiful" package, the bill's sponsors forced their members into a take-it-or-leave-it proposition. There would be no separate votes on the popular parts and the unpopular parts. You were either for the entire agenda or against it. This all-or-nothing approach was designed to forge party discipline and leave little room for dissent. It transformed the vote from a referendum on any single policy into a test of loyalty to the party's broader vision for the country.

The first test of this strategy came in the House of Representatives. With a majority measured in single digits, the leadership had almost no margin for error. The process began in the House Budget Committee, chaired by Representative Jodey Arrington, who formally introduced the bill. From there, it was a furious, week-long campaign of whipping votes, a process of cajoling, persuading, and sometimes threatening members to get them in line. The opposition was united and energized, but the real battle was being fought within the majority party itself.

Two factions proved particularly troublesome. On one side was a small group of fiscal hawks, who were aghast at the bill's projected ten-trillion-dollar addition to the national debt. They had to be convinced that the economic growth spurred by the tax cuts would eventually vindicate their vote. On the other side was a group of moderate members from high-tax suburban districts, who were furious that the bill did not fully repeal the ten-thousand-dollar cap on the State and Local Tax (SALT) deduction. They had to be placated with the compromise of a temporary increase to a forty-thousand-dollar cap, a deal that was hammered out in a series of tense, late-night meetings in the Speaker's office. In the end, the leadership prevailed, pushing the bill through on May 22, 2025, with a nail-biting vote of 215 to 214. One member, signaling their protest, voted "present."

The bill then moved to the far more treacherous waters of the 50-50 Senate, where the Vice President's tie-breaking vote was the only thing giving the majority party control. Here, the reconciliation process kicked into high gear, beginning with the "Byrd Bath." This is the informal name for the process where the Senate Parliamentarian scrubs the bill, listening to arguments from both parties about which provisions violate the Byrd Rule's prohibition on non-budgetary items. Several minor provisions were stripped out at this stage, but the core of the bill—its tax, spending, and entitlement reforms—was deemed compliant and allowed to proceed.

What followed was one of the most grueling and bizarre traditions of the Senate: the "vote-a-rama." Because debate time on a reconciliation bill is strictly limited, senators are instead allowed to offer a virtually unlimited number of amendments, which are then voted on in rapid succession with little to no debate. This process began on the morning of June 30th and raged for twenty-seven consecutive hours. It was a legislative marathon designed to be as painful as possible, a test of physical and mental endurance where senators, fueled by caffeine and sugar, shuffled onto the floor to cast votes on dozens of politically-charged amendments.

The opposition used the vote-a-rama to force the majority to take politically painful votes. They offered amendments to reverse the cuts to Medicaid, to restore the environmental regulations, and to strip out the tax breaks for corporations. Each of these amendments was voted down on a party-line vote, but not before putting vulnerable senators on the record. A few amendments from within the majority party did pass, making minor tweaks to the bill. One such change, for example, slightly increased the funding for rural broadband infrastructure, a key priority for a senator from a sparsely populated state whose vote was considered soft.

As the vote-a-rama exhausted itself in the early afternoon of July 1st, the focus shifted to the handful of senators in the majority who had remained publicly noncommittal. With a 50-50 split, a single defection would kill the entire bill. The party leadership, in coordination with the White House, engaged in a frantic, last-minute burst of deal-making. A senator from a state with a large military presence secured an additional funding boost for a specific shipbuilding program. Another, facing a tough re-election in a state with a large elderly population, won a concession to slightly soften the work requirements for older SNAP recipients. The final holdout, a moderate from a purple state, was brought into line only after a direct call from the President, who reportedly promised to headline a major fundraising event for their campaign.

With every member of the caucus finally accounted for, the Senate moved to a final vote. The chamber was silent as the clerk called the roll. The final tally came in at exactly fifty "ayes" and fifty "nays." All eyes then turned to the Vice President, JD Vance, who, presiding over the Senate, formally cast the tie-breaking fifty-first vote in favor of the bill. The OBBB had cleared its highest hurdle.

But the process was not over. The Senate's version of the bill, with its various amendments, was now different from the one that had originally passed the House. The bill had to return to the lower chamber for one final vote on the amended text. This was a perilous moment. Any of the deals made to win over senators could potentially alienate members in the House. The SALT-focused moderates, in particular, were unhappy that the Senate had not improved upon the forty-thousand-dollar cap.

This is where the full power of the presidency was brought to bear. For the next forty-eight hours, the White House became a command center for the final legislative push. The President and his senior staff worked the phones relentlessly. Lawmakers who were wavering were invited for private meetings at the White House, where they were personally lobbied by the commander-in-chief. Cabinet secretaries were dispatched to Capitol Hill to reassure members about how the bill would benefit their specific districts. The message was clear and direct: a vote against this bill was a vote against the President and the party's entire governing agenda.

The pressure campaign was intense, leaving no stone unturned. The leadership reminded the fiscal hawks that the bill also contained the automatic debt ceiling repeal, a provision many of them saw as a necessary structural reform. They reminded the moderates that while the SALT cap was not fully repealed, the alternative was allowing it to remain at ten thousand dollars. They reminded every member of the popular tax cuts and the military pay raise they would get to campaign on back home. It was a closing argument that focused less on the bill's finer details and more on its overarching political necessity.

The final vote was scheduled for the evening of July 3rd, just before the start of the Independence Day recess. The tension on the House floor was palpable. The leadership knew the vote would be close, and they stationed party whips at every exit to ensure no member left before the vote was called. As the electronic voting board lit up, the "aye" and "nay" columns raced toward the finish line. In the end, the coalition held. The One Big Beautiful Bill passed its final legislative test by a vote of 218 to 214, a slightly larger margin than its first passage, a testament to the effectiveness of the final push. The bill that was once a statement of ambition had now become the law of the land, ready for the President's signature.

CHAPTER TWENTY-FIVE: The "One Big Beautiful Bill" and the Future of America

A piece of legislation is more than the sum of its clauses and appropriations. It is a story, a vision of the society its authors wish to create. The One Big Beautiful Bill, in its immense scope and ambition, is one of the most comprehensive stories ever written into American law. It is a detailed blueprint for a different kind of country, one with a reconfigured relationship between the citizen and the state, a reordered set of national priorities, and a reshaped economic and social landscape. To understand the future envisioned by the OBBB is to understand the fundamental principles that are woven through its thousands of pages, from its sweeping tax reforms to its granular changes in social policy.

At its most fundamental level, the OBBB redefines the American social contract. It redraws the lines that govern what citizens owe the state and what the state, in turn, owes its citizens. The philosophy of taxation, for instance, is decisively shifted. The bill operates on the principle that the income an individual or business earns is fundamentally their own property, and the government's claim on that income should be minimized. The permanent extension of lower tax rates, the creation of new tax-free categories of income like tips and overtime, and the near-elimination of the federal estate tax all reinforce this core idea. This represents a move away from a model where taxes are seen primarily as a tool for funding a broad range of public services and redistributing resources, and toward one where the tax code's primary function is to encourage work, investment, and wealth creation by leaving as much money as possible in private hands.

This redefinition is even more pronounced in the bill's treatment of the social safety net. For sixty years, access to programs like food stamps and Medicaid was based primarily on a calculation of need. The OBBB transforms these programs from entitlements into conditional benefits. The nationwide imposition of strict work requirements for both SNAP and Medicaid eligibility establishes a new, explicit link between public assistance and labor force participation. The bill's subtext is that the government's role is not just to alleviate poverty, but to actively nudge, and in some cases push, able-bodied individuals toward employment. This reflects a fundamental shift in the conceptualization of poverty itself, treating it less as a simple lack of resources and more as a problem that can be addressed through behavioral incentives and mandates designed to promote self-sufficiency.

This new social contract is underwritten by a dramatic reordering of the nation's fiscal and strategic priorities. The OBBB acts as a great sorting mechanism, redirecting hundreds of billions, and ultimately trillions, of dollars from one set of national goals to another. It is a zero-sum game played on a colossal scale. The deep cuts to federal support for renewable energy, public transit, and environmental protection are the necessary financial counterbalance to the massive new investments in the military, border security, and domestic fossil fuel production. The bill makes an unambiguous choice, prioritizing what its authors would define as national sovereignty and physical security over goals like climate change mitigation and the expansion of social welfare programs.

The future America envisioned by the OBBB is one that projects its power through a formidable military and controls its destiny by securing its borders. The trillion-dollar defense budget and the multi-billion-dollar border wall are the twin pillars of this vision. They represent a belief that in a dangerous and competitive world, a nation's strength is measured primarily by its ability to deter and defeat its enemies and to regulate who and what crosses its frontiers. This "peace through strength" and "control through enforcement" model represents a pivot away from an approach that might have placed greater emphasis on diplomacy, foreign aid, and international cooperation as tools of statecraft.

This inward-looking focus is also the driving force behind the bill's economic agenda. The OBBB is a declaration of skepticism toward the globalized economic order that has dominated for the last several decades. The "America First" technology agenda, with its massive government-directed fund and its protectionist undertones, is a deliberate attempt to reshore critical industries and decouple the American innovation ecosystem from its global competitors. The goal is to build a more resilient, self-sufficient national economy, particularly in the high-tech sectors deemed essential for future power. This represents a departure from a decades-long bipartisan consensus that generally favored free trade and open global markets.

The long-term economic landscape that the OBBB seeks to cultivate is one that celebrates the entrepreneur, the risk-taker, and the business owner. The creation of Entrepreneurial Savings Accounts, the enhancement of R&D tax credits, and the permanent relief for "pass-through" businesses are all designed to foster a more dynamic and competitive private sector. The bill places a profound faith in the ability of the market, when unshackled from high taxes and burdensome regulations, to generate prosperity and solve problems. It is a vision that promises greater rewards for success, creating a fertile ground for innovation and wealth creation.

This vision, however, also accepts a harsher reality for those who struggle. The thinning of the social safety net and the emphasis on individual responsibility mean that the consequences of unemployment, illness, or financial distress may be more severe. The America of the OBBB is a place with fewer public guardrails. The shift in federal education funding away from the traditional public school system and toward models of school choice, for example, empowers individual parents but also potentially weakens the universal, communal institution that has been a cornerstone of American society for more than a century. The bill consistently favors individual choice and market-based solutions over public provision and collective security.

This new landscape also implies a significant shift in the physical and industrial geography of the country. The OBBB's massive investment in fossil fuels, commodity agriculture, and defense manufacturing will likely bring a new wave of prosperity to the regions of the country that specialize in these industries. The Rust

Belt may see a resurgence in manufacturing driven by the new technology funds, while the energy-rich states of the South and West are positioned for a boom. Conversely, the states and cities that had bet heavily on a future of green technology, dense urban living, and expanded public transit may find themselves on the losing end of this federal realignment.

The bill also attempts to settle, by legislative force, some of the most contentious cultural debates of the era. The provisions targeting DEI initiatives and mandating certain free speech policies on college campuses are a clear signal that the federal government, under this new philosophy, will not hesitate to intervene in what it views as the excesses of cultural progressivism. The nationwide deportation initiative and the construction of a border wall are not just policy choices; they are powerful statements about national identity and the meaning of citizenship. They paint a picture of an America that is less multicultural and more assimilationist, a nation defined by a shared culture and a common set of laws that are to be strictly enforced.

The OBBB is, in essence, a grand experiment. It is a wager that a society with lower taxes, less regulation, a stronger military, more secure borders, and a leaner social safety net will be a more prosperous, powerful, and virtuous one. It is a bet that the economic growth unleashed by its policies will be so robust that it can overcome the drag of a rapidly rising national debt. It is a confident assertion that the principles of individual responsibility, market competition, and national sovereignty are the surest path to a brighter future.

The changes enacted by this single piece of legislation are so profound and so far-reaching that they will likely define the political and economic terrain for a generation. The bill sets the country on a new trajectory, one that diverges sharply from the path it had been on. The America of 2030 or 2040, should the OBBB's vision come to full fruition, will be a nation that is more inwardly focused, more reliant on its own resources, more skeptical of global cooperation, and more demanding of its own citizens. It will be a country that places a higher premium on strength, security, and individual success, and a lower one on collective social provision and environmental stewardship. The One Big Beautiful Bill is not just a law; it is the opening chapter of a new and uncertain American story.

Made in the USA
Las Vegas, NV
06 July 2025

24493917R00095